Secret Circle of Women

Where Queens Rule
Honey Bees Dance

Laura Henderson

outskirtspress

DENVER, COLORADO

This collection of stories from amazing women is dedicated to my family. To my husband, Richard, our children, Kathryn and Matthew, my Mom and Dad, mother-in-law, Barbara, and of course Grammy Lucy- without all of you, I would not be the woman I am today.
Thank you from the very bottom of my heart.

I also would like to extend my deepest gratitude to the numerous United States Navy Moms who contributed with their most intimate and heartfelt stories - as well as the several other truly amazing women contributors.

Last, but certainly not least, a special thank you to my Cambridge College Professors – especially my first writing instructor – Mary Morrissey who gave me the guidance and inspiration to continue writing.

Your life is defined
By what others achieve
BECAUSE
of you.

~ Laura Henderson

Examine the day
Embrace beauty
Breathe
Pick a flower
Look at the gentle leaves
And Petals
All uniquely different
Formed from soil, water, sun
A kaleidoscope of color
For your eyes only.

~ Laura Henderson

Bring yourself to a point of full beauty and potential
Imagine your life in vivid colors
Take a step back
Admire the wonder of life.

~ Laura Henderson

Table of Contents

Preface

There is only one Queen in a hive ~
The Queen rules.

Female bees spend the first half of their lives working inside the hive. The worker bee tends to the Queen's every need while carefully guarding the hive. They do it in one of the most well organized societies. Their mission is to prepare the cells ahead of the Queen, keep her dry, fed, comfortable, and clean. The Queen's health and well-being is vital to the hive community. Once fed a diet of "royal jelly", the Queen performs "magic" by laying eggs. This triggers the morphological changes that make the rest of her life possible. So, what is the waggling "honey bee dance" all about? The eccentric "circle dance" is performed to alert the other bees in the hive of food sources nearby by guiding them to the perfect flower. Bees have their own unique communication system with intense laser accuracy using sound, scent, angle and timing. The most particular flowers aid in the magical transformation producing a delightful, delectable sweetness - Honey.

Honey has been around for centuries and can last forever. Honey is pure, complete and eternal. What a fantastical journey into the depths of humankind from a source so simple to imagine. The bee does not rest or pause, but keeps doing her delicate work in perfect harmony with her only one true goal in mind at that very moment. Women, like bees, possess a memory of time that allows us to navigate through each day without a single thought. We are truly amazing!

Introduction

She headed straight toward the garage door like a "bat out of hell". I sat on the passenger's side pressing my foot on the floor hoping to break the speed. Luckily, with precision accuracy, she always managed to "clear" the sides and stop the car inches from the back of the garage.

As I reflect on this childhood memory, I realize the unequivocal significance of time and family. Just like honey, memories last forever!

It has been twenty-three years since I last walked into the Bennett Street kitchen, but I still have a vivid recollection of once glancing over at the vintage oven that resembled a "Pandora's Box" filled with fabulous delicacies. The mouth-watering aromas that once filled the room were distinctly comparable to an authentic North End trattoria. Those smells take me back to a place where memories of a lifetime were created. Grammy Lucy, the untamed driver, always had a homemade Italian dish warming in that oven when I visited - zucchini, meatballs, pasta fagioli and gnocchi. My favorite treats were the pastries shaped like bow ties, generously sprinkled with powered sugar and then smothered with pure honey. The taste of this sweetness on my tongue is a remembrance of a time gone by which I will forever cherish.

Within that little Hive
Such Hints of Honey lay
As made Reality a Dream
And Dreams, Reality
-- Emily Dickinson

It is abundantly clear that this journey of self- discovery starts at mid-life. What is it about mid-life that makes one so driven to meet life-long unachieved goals and eventually become a turning point for amazing achievements? Is it the actual number; 40, 45, 50 - or is it more than that? We push through the power of time by developing our inner being where we now have the wisdom to move ahead. Some say it could be that mid-point in a woman's life when she realizes that her reproductive clock has struck its last note. I define mid-life as finally breaking out and realizing the power to be you. Freedom can be exhilarating when one is more comfortable in her own body.

Women share the same common "Secret".

Purity ~ Like Honey~ is Fabulous,
Transparent and Absolute.

1
Inspiration

What defines "Amazing" women who have accomplished or overcome "Amazing" things by mid-life? This book showcases a collection of stories from 50 remarkable women that I am sure will give you a better understanding of what one may characterize as "Amazing". Some stories will absolutely shock you, some will surprise you, and others will bring you to tears. I had such a fabulous outpouring of responses because I realize how many people enjoy hearing inspirational, real-life stories. Sometimes hearing other people's life stories sheds light on the possibilities of life, and allows us to develop empathy and humility in these crazy times. Perhaps you will walk away with a broadened sense of vision after reading this book. Women from all over the U.S. shared their stories for this book. In most cases, only their first names have used to honor their sense of anonymity.

I have wanted to write an inspirational book for several years. I struggled with a specific style that would absolutely intrigue others. The epiphany came one evening just after midnight. That evening was the night before I was to give the Cambridge College Graduation Commencement Address in front of nearly 3000 people. I thought; why not write about amazing accomplishments of women my age! Some may say I am bragging here, but I had just turned 50, graduated with honors, and now the idea of delivering my "speech of a lifetime" in front of the entire graduating class was truly amazing to me. I stepped out of my comfort zone and was ready to go BIG!

Since that day, I have grown in so many ways, and reflections on my own life allowed me to see a clear vision of the future. An important lesson learned is that time is non-negotiable! By sharing unique stories collected from other women across America, one can see many similarities - as well as begin to understand the events and circumstances that some women live through each and everyday of their lives. Collectively, we have accomplished so much, but there is still so much to do!

Know your purpose in life against which you will measure all decisions.

How does one achieve this?
Start by asking yourself:

~ **"Who am I at the core?"** ~

~ **"What do I stand for?"** ~

~ **"Why does it matter?"** ~

Once you have answered these questions, you will be true to yourself, true to your passions, and realize the potential you have to achieve greatness.

What gives one the motivation to move ahead in life? How does a woman overcome life's biggest challenges and step out of that closed box to spread her Queen wings to infinity?

Here is what I live by:
Be true to yourself.
Expand your opportunities.
Embrace change.
Embrace change.
Set your own compass.
Release negativity
Challenge yourself fully.
Set your own standards.

There are so many amazing and inspirational stories in this book, but one comes to mind for me in a statement one woman made when I asked her to describe what age 50 meant to her. She said she is "Better able to cultivate friendships", and proved that sexual attractiveness does not end once a woman passes a set number of years. Janet is able to focus on her needs by feeling better about herself and getting into better shape both physically and mentally. With this comes a heightened sense of self-esteem and self-awareness, a quality that is attractive at any age. She said, "Because she is so comfortable with her body and confidence at this age, she often feels like she could express her feelings so freely without worrying what others may say."

Be You

~

Be Free

~

Be Unique

Possibilities are endless if you set your own compass!

There is only one Queen.

"When you bring your full attention to each moment, a day is a complete lifetime of living and learning. You must prepare your mind, body and spirit. In this way, your destiny is in your control."
Mark Divine

2
Amazing Women
in History

Epic Women in History Who Blew It Out Of the Water!

50-Barbra Streisand won a 10-year film and recording contract estimated at $60 million.

40- Joan Ganz Cooney founded Children's Television Workshop and became the mastermind behind "Sesame Street."

40-Harriet Beecher Stowe, a mother of six who occasionally wrote for magazines, published Uncle Tom's Cabin, an antislavery novel of such force that it is generally recognized as one of the causes of the Civil War.

42-Arlette Rafferty Schweitzer became the first woman to give birth to her own grandchildren.

49-Julia Child published her book: *Mastering the art of French cooking.*

50-Terri Tapper became the oldest female certified kite board instructor in the USA and possibly the world.

59-Clara Barton founded the American Red Cross.

80 - Grandma Moses (Anna Mary Robertson Moses)
Anna was a renowned American folk artist. Grandma Moses first came to public attention in 1940, at the age of 80. She began painting in her seventies after abandoning a career in embroidery because of arthritis

95 - Nola Hill Ochs became a Guinness World Record holder as the world's oldest college graduate. The 95-year old graduated from Fort Hays State University in Kansas 77 years after she first started taking classes. She earned a general studies degree with an emphasis in history, graduating alongside her grand daughter who was 21 years old at the time.

"Ordinary people accomplishing extraordinary things. We're all extraordinary in our own way, and that it's what we do with our extraordinariness that sets us apart and makes all the difference."
~Denzel Washington

3
Stories from Amazing Women

Get Ready.

Fasten your seatbelt!

Darlene - Raymond, NH

My name is Darlene. In 1966, I was conceived during a brutal rape. My 15-year-old mom was so traumatized that she did not speak of it for two years. She preferred people think she was promiscuous rather than relive the horror of the rape when she realized she was pregnant with me. She married under social pressure. For the next two years, he raped her until she was pregnant again and on the verge of suicide. Divorced, we moved to her moms.

My mom could not fathom that he would abuse small children. My sister and I were sent to spend weekends with our father's mother, who was complicit in his crimes against women and children. We were taught to keep silent about the abuse as toddlers, but acted out in various ways; getting in trouble, nightmares, illness, having accidents, defiant attitudes and fights.

My mom was oblivious of our father's abuse of us and sent my sister to live with his new family. After a visit there, I insisted she rescue my sister, but they did not get along. So, my sister went to live with my mom's mother. We were terribly poor. We lived with other family members for months at a time. It was chaotic. There was a lot of alcohol and prescription drug use among the family.

At thirteen, I was molested by an uncle from my mom's side and my life spiraled out of control; fighting all the time, running away, drinking, drugging and desperate. I was quickly the target of traffickers. First sold on my fourteenth birthday, a quagmire of rape, kidnapping, abuse and vagrancy began. At seventeen, I was sold to a small-time loan shark. He held me in an apartment as his house pet. I felt safer. He dressed me up and took me out to dinners. There would be no more beatings, rapes, diseases or bugs.

He told me that if I got pregnant I would have to have an abortion. I had been purchased numerous times a day for most of the last four years, so I did not think there was much of a threat. I got so sick; I went to the emergency room where they did a pregnancy test. Of course, I had to tell him I was pregnant. He slammed his fist on the table and said, "I want no life!" That shook me to the core. I walked around the apartment after he left throwing my hands up in the air and asking if God would help me. I had a supernatural dream of the abortion procedure in living color from the perspective of inside the womb. I had no way of imagining the detail and level of development that I saw. It was accurate. I called a social worker who had connected with me as a runaway. She found a home that would take me in.

At dinner with him after the appointment, I pretended to have had the abortion. It was not terribly difficult because the dream was so raw. I was terrified that he would find out. I was shaking and distant. I cried. I went to the bathroom frequently to be convincing. It worked and he let me go. Saving my baby, saved my life.

After a while, I too lived with my mom's mother. She helped me with my daughter and I went to nursing school right away after I got my GED. I had not gone to one day of high school. I met Mark when my daughter was six months old. We had a rocky start. I still had many issues from all of the abuse and did not believe that I was good enough for Mark or anyone else.

When I graduated Nursing school, we were not seeing each other. I got pregnant again. The father wanted nothing to do with me, but Mark asked me to marry him while I was pregnant. He had asked three times. I refused him. I still could not trust anyone. After my second daughter was born, I asked him to marry me.

We married. I focused on my children and learning all that I could about how the Bible tells us to live. I read many books on healing wounded hearts and leadership. I provided home education for all of my five children from 1990 through 2013. This gave me the ability to work on myself and formulate their educational pursuits to meet their individual needs and strengths. We all came through the years with confidence, a strong work ethic and empathy.

I started my property management company in 2008. I have purchased, sold, rehabbed and rented property. I taught real estate acquisition strategies for a couple of years too. I still work as a nurse, as well.

Business is a fantastic personal growth mechanism. I encourage people to find their strengths and talents and use them to produce well in the world. Everyone has special gifts to share and a unique purpose on earth.

I have been married for almost 25 years. My eldest owns her own salon. My second daughter, a homemaker, has two beautiful children. My third child, a son, owns residential real estate, has a full time job, and is earning a degree in finance. My fourth child, a girl, owns her own domestic services business; cleaning houses, caring for children and training animals. My fifth works in retail selling high-end gadgets and teaches self-defense for his friends.

I am a strong advocate for pregnant women and trafficking victims. Preserving the lives of mother and child in crisis situations is definitely a calling to which I am uniquely suited. I speak at youth groups, young adult groups, banquets and other events. I also do radio and television interviews to inspire people to help and offer hope. I run a nonprofit in my state. I also have a speaking business; *theDarlingPrincess.com* to reveal that bad beginnings do not necessitate bad endings.

Jennifer - Lusby, MD

I am Jennifer. In 1991, I embarked on a journey that would lead me into an illustrious career serving in the United States

Navy. I served my country proudly for 21 years (September 23, 1991 to April 30, 2013) retiring as a Chief Petty Officer (E-7).

In the first four years of my Naval career I was an Ocean Systems Technical Analyst (OTA). My job entailed detecting, localizing and tracking enemy submarines. Wanting to try something different, I eventually signed up for and went through the Naval Aircrew Candidate training in Pensacola, Florida in 1995. One of my greatest accomplishments was being among the elite few to graduate from this school. Surprisingly, I was the first African American female in over five years to complete this training!

For over 14 years as an Aircrewman, I flew on three different platforms (E6-A, P-3 and EP-3), flew in combat missions in support of three wars (Kosovo, Afghanistan and Iraq), logged over 3700 flight hours and received four Air Medals. I also proudly knocked down stereotypes by becoming the first African American female Aircrewman, the first African American Aircrewman in the enlisted ranks and the first female In Flight Technician during my squadron tours.

My distinguished military career didn't stop there, as I changed my focus in the military to Active Duty welfare and completed the Substance Abuse and Rehabilitation Program School in Point Loma, CA 2010. In December 2011, I became a certified Alcohol and Drug Counselor (ADCI).

I reaped the rewards of working hard, helping others and being a role model. I earned numerous personal achievements and awards including Outstanding Military Person of the Year (an honor recognized by the Washington State Masons), 2007 Naval Air Station Whidbey Island Sea Sailor of the Year, two Navy and Marine Corps Commendation Medals, five Navy and Marine Corps Achievement Medals as well as other unit and campaign awards. In March 2012, I earned an Associate of Science in Business Administration Degree from Columbia College of Missouri. Here I remain as an active Alumnus.

My true destiny is motivational speaking. My first opportunity came during an African American month celebration in 2005 when I spoke in front of 100 people. Since then, I have delivered numerous other speeches for cultural events and at Inglewood Community Adult School in CA. This is where I spoke to over 200 inner city school students delivering the following message: "No matter what you want to do in life, do your very best at it and never let anyone discourage you from achieving your dreams." I really like to keep it real when delivering my messages.

Recently, I published my first book titled; Tomorrow My Sunshine Will Come: Memoirs of Women Who Survived Domestic Violence. I am also an active member of National Association of Professional Women (NAPW) , Toastmaster International, and the proud Founder and Chief Executive Officer of Inspirationally Speaking, LLC as well as Founder of the Unstoppable You Women's Conference. Besides that, I am the co-host for The Journey: Meeting of the Minds, which broadcasts weekly on YouTube and WBNDRADIO.com.

Additionally, I am currently attending University of Maryland University College in pursuit of a Bachelor's Degree in Communications. My accomplishments are living proof that dreams, passions and goals are obtainable if you trust in God, surround yourself with positive people, and put one foot in front the other.

Maria - Methuen, MA

I do believe everyone has a story of heartache and everyone has crosses to bear and although I have been blessed in many ways, I have had more than my fair share of tragedy.

I was raised as an only child in a middle class family whose parents were divorced by the time I was about nine years old. Although I attempted to live a normal childhood I was somehow always sheltered due to the fear most of my family had of the terrible things that can happen in this world.

I lived with my mother but saw my dad often. The roles they played in my life were very different. My mother was the "security blanket" who took care of my fears and was very giving in monetary and emotional ways. My Dad was the one who did many sports and outdoor activities with me. Now looking back, I realize a lot of my fear and worry came from my upbringing - I was subliminally "taught" that the world was a scary place when not in the presence of my parents.

When I was 18, my mother divorced her second husband. At that point, my mother, my best friend and I took a three-week vacation to California. They both loved California and my mother told me she wanted to move there. I laughed it off knowing she could never leave me or live without me for I was her life. I believe to this day that she honestly thought I would move to the West coast with her, but I had a new job and boyfriend, and all my other family and friends here so I decided to stay back. I will never forget the day she moved away. I distinctively remember she had a white shirt on and

I cried so hard all my eye makeup ran all over it. I couldn't believe it, she was really leaving, never in my life had I ever felt so alone as when I watched vehicle drive away.

We spoke all the time on the phone. We even bought video phones way before you could Skype on the internet. She would come back to visit every year for my birthday to spend it with me and to partake in her annual traditions back in Massachusetts. It was funny, not only did she worry about me being here alone; I worried about everything that could happen to her in California. I can remember being nauseous when the news spoke of earthquakes, the Los Angeles riots or just her being a woman alone in a large city. We had a private joke of telling each other, "Wear your seat belt, Chew your food well -Love ya". I even bought a programmable teddy bear for her that had my voice saying those very words.

Throughout my childhood, flying was something my mom was terrified of doing. I remember she went to Italy when I was very young with my grandmother. To put it lightly, she was a mess. I still can't believe she actually got on the plane and went.

She lived in California for almost 15 years so the only way she could realistically come back to visit was flying, but each time she was scared. That fear never seemed to dissipate. I have flown a few times in my life but I think, because I saw my mom's fear of flying, it was not something I ever enjoyed.

What does this have to do with anything you may ask? Well, let me tell you. My mom came back in September 2001 for my birthday as she always did, but this year was different. My husband and I have taken on the task of caring for un-adoptable animals and this limits our vacation time because they are in need of special care. Because of this, my husband and I never got to go on a formal honeymoon after our marriage in 1999. We thought it would be great idea to go for part of my mom's visit knowing how much she loved animals and we trusted her to care for them. I can remember the call from her telling me the dates she booked her flight to come here and I was disappointed because I would not have enough time to spend with her if I was incorporating my own trip into this period. She ended up calling me back to tell me that she changed her flight from Sunday September 9 to Tuesday September 11. The best news was my mother actually said she was thinking of coming back to live on the East coast and I was thrilled. She even sent out her resume to local companies.

I remember being so happy to see her smiling face with her arms wide open to hug me when she stepped off the plane. We spent the rest of our vacation time doing our annual traditions - the Feast of the Three Saints, visiting relatives, shopping, going out to eat and just making my birthday a special day for me. On the morning of 9/11 my Mom got up to get ready for her flight back to California and I was lying in bed, sad that she was leaving and that I had to go back to work that day since my vacation was now over.

I got out of bed to say our goodbyes...we hugged and kissed. I then crawled back into bed because I had a little time left to sleep.

Now it was time for her to leave so she came into my room to give me a final hug and kiss, told me not to cry and that she loved me. As I laid in bed the last and final words we spoke was me saying, " Wear your seat belt" and she replied

;"And chew your food well - Love ya" - we both kind of giggled and she closed my bedroom door behind her. I began my drive to work on that beautiful clear fall day, thinking that at least it was a good day for my mother to fly since there was no bad weather in the forecast. About an hour later while sitting at my desk I took a call from someone yelling into the phone at me. "Where is your Mother"? I was confused and did not even know how to answer. My cousin told me a plane had just hit a building in NYC followed that. My husband had driven her to the airport that morning, so with my heart racing and my hands shaking I tried to call my husband at work. I was trying not to be hysterical but I needed to know what flight she was on.

He finally remembered that it was United 175, and for a split second, I was relieved because I knew that was not the plane that had hit the first tower. This almost immediately changed when a co-worker came in our office to inform us that another plane, Flight 175, had struck the second tower. I became weak and slightly panic stricken but still believed this could not be true. A few kind people at work helped me. One drove my car and another drove me to my great aunts house to be close to family. From that moment on, I was in denial. I refused to watch the news and avoided the TV and newspapers like the plague. To this day, I have only seen footage related to 9/11 by accident. I can only remember bits and pieces of those days, months and even years to follow. I believe it was my mind's way of protecting me from that horrific event. I was sure that September 11, 2001 was going to be my demise. As I said, I do not remember a lot but I do remember my cries, screams and literally begging my husband to kill me. It sounds so dramatic, but that was honestly, what I prayed for. I was a zombie for years. I can't even tell you much more, other than I went into a deep depression, maintained my denial, and was extremely overwhelmed by the events and tasks that needed to be completed. Between my work, her work, her home, her cats, her body not being found, paperwork for Massachusetts, New York and California, the press, the FBI, the airlines, and the sea of calls and visits from people. My private horror had become a public one that will forever change the course of history. It also changed my history. My last day at work was 9/11 and I never stepped foot in that building again. There were people and friends I worked with for over 13 years that I never got to say goodbye to so it was just too painful to go back. I became withdrawn, gained 80 lbs, and developed severe anxiety. I was basically just surviving. I always considered my dad and I close but he really stepped up to the plate after 9/11 and we became closer than ever. I was so grateful to have him in my life.

Unfortunately, my seemingly healthy father died suddenly in 2008 and once again, there was no chance to say goodbye. I was devastated.

The only two people who loved me unconditionally were gone and I was alone, truly alone. Normally by this time in my life, I would have considered having children with my husband but I was unable to function let alone raise a child. In 2008, I actually talked to my Dad about possibly adopting and he seemed quite excited, but with his sudden death, I was once again thrown into a deep depression.

I did realize however, that my window of having a child in my life was closing due to my age, as we all know time does not stand still. I made the bold decision that I wanted a child, someone to love, someone to share my history and memories of my mother and father.

So, this is when the miracle that turned my life around made me want to live for the first time in eight years. I really wanted to live.

If anyone knows anything about adoption, it can be a long drawn out process so we started, prepared to wait through the months or even years, it could take. A few weeks later I decided to call the adoption agency to make sure they received all our required paperwork only to be told that there was a couple who was considering us to adopt their child who was due less than five weeks! Our prayers were answered -we were chosen and going to be parents in less than a month! This is unheard of from what we have been told.

As most parents often say my life was never the same after my child was born, this was now true on so many levels. For the first time in my life, I honestly believed in miracles.

We got in the car with our hastily purchased baby equipment and drove to Ohio just in time for the birth of our child. I was never so grateful to any human being for giving us such a priceless gift.

Here we are five years later and our daughter, Isabella is truly an amazing child. There is something very special about her -she is like an old soul. She is smart, kind, beautiful, funny and like no other, I have met. Remember she is a miracle. No matter what life hands me - good or bad, I thank God each day for this precious gift. This child has made me appreciate everything in my life, she is the reason I want to live.

She is my gift from my parents.

Ruth - Bethel, Oklahoma

I was 38 years old and a single parent working at a job that I could not explain to other people without having their eyes glaze over. I was essentially ordering reports from the Data Processing department in Los Angeles for an office in Atlanta. We got a midrange computer in our office and I decided that I could do my job better if I taught myself to program and ran some of the reports on our office computer. I borrowed a COBOL book and got busy figuring out how to write programs. I was very successful at mastering COBOL and improving efficiency in our office.

Our company decided that they wanted to centralize and picked Dallas, TX as the location. I decided I would only move to Dallas if given a programming position. In spite of my success in Atlanta, I had a hard time convincing the interviewers that I knew what I was doing. I was pretty upset when told I would not be considered for a position as an application programmer, but the head of the production programming department was willing to take a chance on me. Sadly, for a move all the way from Atlanta to Dallas I was only offered a $2000/year raise. I almost did not take it. When I got to Dallas, it did not take me long to prove myself. The Department Director had decided to switch from COBOL programming to RPG and had arranged classes for us. I was "lucky" enough to find myself with the Director, as well as some top application programmers. I held my own. It was only a short time before I was showing other programmers how to do the job. After I had been there about seven or eight months they realized that there were issues with salary equity and made an adjustment. I got a $24,000/year raise. I was eventually promoted to Senior Programmer Analyst and allowed to work on a virtual basis. I moved to Oklahoma and essentially just made trips to Dallas every couple of months for meetings.

While living in Oklahoma, I got a phone call from the Director. He told me that the applications department wanted to have his best programmer. "That would be you," he said. When I said I wouldn't move back, he said, "I guess I will call my second best programmer." She was living in Longview, Texas and didn't want to move either. The applications folks decided that they really wanted me, so I finally got into that department. Although I did not get the promotion, I became an acting technical lead, someone who guided less experienced programmers, led projects, and did code reviews.

Our biggest competitor purchased the company and then I became a schoolteacher.

Peggy - Larkspur, CO

In June 1994, I was volunteering at Fort Hood's thrift- store intake room. My husband had agreed to meet me there at lunchtime. Around noon, I looked up and saw him sitting in a chair next to a pile of clothes. We smiled at each other and I indicated that I wouldn't be too much longer. A few minutes later, I looked for him. He was not there.

Introductions: My name in Peggy and my husband is Byron. We have been married for five very happy years. Byron is a Captain in the Army. I am a stay-at-home mom for two beautiful children, Kenneth age 4 and Cassie age 3. Byron and I are very happy with our lives and the path we are on. We are Sunday school teachers at the chapel on post. Raising our kids is a blast. Everything was perfect.

I looked in every room at the thrift store, thinking Byron was browsing the store while waiting. I couldn't find him. I waited around for 30 minutes then decided he must have gone back to work. I went to the daycare and picked up my kids then drove home. On the way, I saw Bryon driving the opposite direction on the divided highway. That is odd, where had he been? I drove on home. I was already worried and confused, but when I got home, I got downright scared. I could tell Byron had been there. The front door was standing open. Our two dogs were running around the neighborhood. I collected the dogs, fed the kids their lunch then put them down for a nap.

I called Byron's office. His top sergeant answered the phone. I learned that Byron had been gone for a few hours. It had been almost two hours since I saw him on the highway. Top shared with me that Byron had been acting strangely, not focused, pre-occupied and not making a whole lot of sense during conversations. Top asked me if Byron had been drinking. I told him no, that's not possible. That is not something we do except at social functions. Top said he would have to report Byron AWOL (absence without leave) soon. I panicked. I asked him not to. Just give Byron the afternoon to come back.

He agreed. He would report Byron at 4:00pm if he had to. I thanked him and hung up.

I did not know what to do. There was no one else I could call. Doing so could threaten Byron's career. I could not chance that. When I am upset I clean so that's what I started doing. I am moving around the house in a light daze. I took a trash bag out to the garage. When I opened the trash bin, I looked inside as I swung the bag in. I gasped and jumped back. There was a bible lying on top of the other bags, many of its pages were burned. Byron! What is happening? Where are you? I started crying. I ran in to the house and called Top.

Within minutes of Top calling the military police (MP) and Byron's chain of command a search of the post and the surrounding area was launched to look for Byron. The command's chaplain and Top Walker came to my home. One of them called my good friend and neighbor and asked her to help with the kids while I answered questions. I did not have many answers. I was as clueless as they were. Hours passed, I kept my kids routine as much as I could. They were confused about the strangers in our home and wanted their daddy. No one left my side. At 1:00am, I could not go any more. My friends persuaded me to go to bed. They would stay up and promised to come get me with any updates. I crawled into bed with Kenneth and fell asleep.

At 5:00am, the phone rang and woke me up. It was my mom. She wanted to know if Byron had come home. She said she was going to drive up when I told her he had not. She would see me in about four hours. I thanked her and hung up. My friends were all sitting in the living room. They had been up all night. They stayed until my mom got there. Shortly after my mom arrived, I got a call from a friend who lived across town. She had just gotten back from running errands. Her kids went into their backyard and found Byron's BDU uniform jacket on the ground. My friend went out to look around. She found Byron's wedding ring on the ground close to where her kids found the jacket. When she saw Byron's last name on the jacket she called me wondering why it was there. I filled her in on what was happening. Now, I am beside myself. I am almost hysterical.

The rest of the day is a blur. We doted on the kids by keeping ourselves busy - doing whatever we could think of just to make it through each hour. I was sick with worry. I remember someone, perhaps an MP, stopping by the house for a change of clothes for Byron in case they needed them. I did not have the strength to question them- I just did it. The phone rang often. Fellow command wives, friends, relatives asking if anything had changed. At 7:00pm, I got a call from an MP. He told me Byron had been found. He asked how fast I could get to the post hospital. Byron was going to be transported there and would be there in about 20 minutes. I was there before he was.

Byron was dressed in the shorts and tee shirt I had provided. I ran to him and hugged him. His reaction stunned me. He reacted appropriately, hugging me back but I could tell he was not sure who I was. He recognized me as someone important to him but he didn't know why. We walked into the hospital escorted by several MP's and started a 30 day rehabilitation plan on the psychiatric ward.

An exam room is where we were taken. Two doctors were already there. They asked Byron to sit down and asked me to sit down in a chair just behind him so that the doctor could see me too. He asked Byron questions, "What is your name? Where do you live? Do you know where you are? What are your kid's names? Who are your parents, siblings?" The questions went on and on for hours. The doctor would glance at me with each answer looking for indication if the answers were right or wrong. Byron answered wrong many times. Byron was admitted to the hospital. After a careful examination lasting several hours, the doctors told me Byron was suffering from a mental illness called Bi-polar. I was shaken. I had heard that term before. All I knew about Bi-polar was what I had seen in movies or from stories I had heard. This could not be. In my mind, Byron had a nervous breakdown! He was not mentally ill! I plunged deep into denial. All I could think of was that Byron's brilliant career was over. What would happen to him? Would he ever be the same? The proverbial carpet was yanked out from under our world.

I blamed doctors for diagnosing him too fast. How could they be sure? Over the next several days I became more educated about Byron's illness and the truth of what was happening began to take down the walls of denial I was clinging to so desperately.

Byron remembers everything he did during the day and a half he was gone. He says he remembers going through the motions but he felt he was an observer of his actions. He had no conscious thought what he was doing or going to do next. We talked about his hours away from home. He remembered going to my friend's house just to visit her but she was not home.

There was nothing else significant that had happened

before he was found. He drove around not conscious of the road, laws, or even looking before entering an intersection. God was guiding him so he wasn't worried. He slept in the car for several hours. Eventually, he became very thirsty. He was in the country somewhere and found a house. He walked up to the door and knocked. No one answered but there were older children inside. They called their mom at work and told her there was a stranger outside. She called the police and my husband had been brought home.

Over the first week Byron was in the hospital I started to understand why the doctors gave the diagnosis they did. I was confused, worried and scared. Byron was talking non-sense. He said every human had more than one soul. He even pointed out to me where he thought they were with our bodies. He had grandiose thoughts that he had the power to access and push the "dooms day" button. He talked about God a lot. Doctors told me that these topics were not unusual. I thought about what he had done to his bible. When I asked him about it, he solemnly said that he was angry and thought, in that moment, that all in the bible was a lie. My heart broke for him. He looked so sad. I don't remember exactly, but I'd like to think we hugged at that moment and held on tight.

I would go home from the hospital exhausted each day. Byron's family and my family were all in town by this time. My children and I were well taken care of and supported but life was so surreal and no one could tell me what was going to happen. How could they? In a short time, I developed a new routine. I would spend every visiting hour I could with Byron and the rest of the time I would be at home trying to keep life as normal as I could for Kenneth and Cassie. The prescribed medications and hours of therapy started to transform Byron back to his new normal. After 30 days in the hospital, he was released. It was a great homecoming. The kids were so happy to have their daddy home. We all were.

Byron never went back to work for his beloved Army. We had a reduced income that forced me to find a job. I hadn't worked outside the home in over five years. I was fortunate and found a job as a secretary. Try as I may, I cannot remember what the business was! That few months on the job are a blur because all I really did was worry about Byron and the kids. Byron stayed home with them but he wasn't completely well and I worried he'd fall asleep or not notice if one of the kids was getting into something they shouldn't. After a short while, I began to relax about that, but just a little.

A couple of weeks after I started working, Byron started to complain about intense pain in his abdomen. He would pace the floors at night and lie on the couch during the day unable to move around very well. Every test known to man was run on him. All of the results came back unremarkable. There was no physical reason for the pain. There was nothing else that could have been done.

Over the next weeks, Byron applied and interviewed for jobs close in our area. He flew to nearby large cities and interviewed through job fairs. There were many promising options and some big companies like Motorola and IBM were interested in him. We felt confident that he could have been offered a job. However, the pain Byron was suffering would keep him awake all night. He could not focus on his interviews from lack of sleep. Other times, he would be fidgeting in his seat trying to conceal the pain that completely shattered his chances of a successful interview. Byron would come home completely devastated. He was consumed with worry. How was he going to support his family? What would happen once the Army released him? Why was Byron in so much physical pain? There were so many questions and we didn't have any answers.

As if we were not coping with enough, I found out I was pregnant. While we were very happy about the news, it clearly was not the time to prepare for a baby! Christmas was fast approaching and Byron's military benefits were just as quickly running out. I finally convinced Byron to go back to the doctor. He made the appointment. He got an appointment within a couple of days.

Byron came home for that doctor's appointment a furious mess. I had never seen him so worked up and angry. He spat out that the doctor told him his pain was. He said it was psychosomatic; it was all in his mind! He said it was all he could do not to lay that guy out flat on his back. He kept saying that this was ridiculous and this could not possibly be true. He said that there was something wrong with him and the doctors could not figure it out so they came up with "this garbage." I consoled him the best I could. I had to wonder if this was true. He was under a lot of stress. At first, stress manifested itself into a Bi-polar episode but medication was keeping that under control. What if stress was finding a different way to attack his body? I gently shared this idea but Byron dismissed it. I allowed him.

It was February when Byron scheduled a local interview with a company based in Indianapolis, Indiana. It was a food manufacturing company looking for a project manager. Byron had strong skills as a manager, but had never worked in this industry. We only had a month left of military benefits. My pay wasn't enough to sustain us and Byron had few options. The company offered Byron the job a few days later! We were ecstatic! He would report to work in two weeks.

There wasn't enough time to pack up, to sell the house, and everything else it took to move a family of four. Byron and I decided it would be best for him to fly out to Indianapolis now so that he would have time to find a place to live and get settled before starting his job. He was still fighting with pain and wanted time to find his footing.

We traveled to my parents' home the day before Byron left. I needed a break before tackling all this moving stuff. I was overwhelmed. I felt trouble brewing with my pregnancy. I knew that if I mentioned this to Byron he would not leave. That was not an option. We were lucky to get this job and I wasn't going to let anything jeopardize it. Byron got to Indianapolis safely. He said he thought I would really like it there and had found a nice apartment he thought the kids would love. There was a big pond with lots of trees and "forest life" in them. There were strolling paths and many geese. He sounded positive and I thought I heard a smile in his voice. This is good. The next day I went to the doctor concerned about my pregnancy. While I was at the hospital, I suffered a miscarriage. After testing, the doctor determined that the cause was due to stress. I was so sad. I made myself find strength through the thought that everything happens for a reason. I may never know why, but these things happening in my life were out of my hands. I leaned on my faith that I, we, were going to get through all of this and that life would be good again, some day. To say the least, Byron was very upset with me for allowing him to leave when I knew there was trouble, but he eventually understood why I did it and forgave me.

Over the next month, I wrapped things up with the house, got everything shipped off to Indianapolis then drove the kids and I back to my parents' home for a quick good bye. My mom wouldn't hear of me driving for 20 plus hours with the kids. So she drove up to Indianapolis with me and then flew back home. We had an amazing road trip! We got to see Graceland, in Memphis, drove through the Shenandoah Mountains, and we sang silly kid songs while eating a year's supply of junk food in the four days we took to get there. The kids and I had a great reunion with Byron. We were together again. I could see some of the good coming back. Without explanation, the pain Byron was suffering gradually faded until it was gone. It is hard to admit but that doctor was right. Byron knows that pain was real and was caused by overwhelming stress and worry. His mind conjured that overload into his abdomen as pain. We have learned that stress can do some crazy things to the body. We also learned that abdominal pain is a preferable symptom to what could have been. Stress can be deadly.

We started our new lives in Indianapolis. We lived in the apartment Byron picked out for a year. The kids and I spent a lot of time strolling around the "woods" and playing near the pond. The kids learned to keep their distance from the geese but they always enjoyed watching them. We bought a new home on the northwest side of Indianapolis. It was an adorable little 3-bedroom nestled up to trees and a little brook. It was perfect!

We celebrated that Christmas in Colorado with some of Byron's family. They were thrilled to see their son was healthy and happy once again. We had a wonderful time. A few days after getting home from our trip to Colorado, we found out I was pregnant again! Oh, what a shocking and joyous day that was! Even the kids were excited at the prospect of a new baby brother or sister. It didn't take me long to get over my shock and join my kids in their excitement.

Five months into my pregnancy, I went into labor. I was rushed to the hospital where the doctors were able to stop the labor. Doctors didn't know why this had happened, but they told me I had to go on complete bed rest for the duration of my pregnancy. I remember laughing aloud. I reminded them I had a 4 and 5 year old at home. They didn't join me in my amusement. This was serious. I wised up and took their words to heart. I called my mom that night; I told her what happened and hoped that she would understand that I had already booked a flight for the next day to send my kids to her for a while. She never blinked. She just asked what time she had to be at the airport.

Just before my pregnancy problems began, Byron had become unhappy with his job. He had worked hard to learn the business and did an outstanding job. He wasn't being challenged anymore. There was nowhere else to go within the small company. Byron was very grateful to them for giving him a chance almost two years before. He couldn't bring himself to let them down by leaving for a job he really wanted. He wanted to be a system's engineer with an aerospace company. That was what his education and military training had prepared him for. He was still struggling with his conscious when he flew to Denver, Colorado to interview for a job as a systems engineer. He was offered the job. I hadn't seen him this excited about anything in a very long time. It really was a great opportunity, one that motivated him to leave the company that gave him his life back.

Byron had to report to his new job at the beginning of August, which was only three weeks away. I couldn't do any because of my restrictions. Byron had to work to train his replacement. We decided to leave everything as it was and worry about the house after the baby was born. We had to be geographically separated again to accommodate the COBRA medical coverage we had. Bryon would start his new job and I would stay with my parents. I was happy to be with my children again.

I went into labor about three weeks later. I had little warning. My mom rushed me to the hospital. She went into the emergency room with me. She settled me into a wheel chair and ran back outside to park her vehicle. When she got back, I was already in an ER room in hard labor. My little girl was born less than five minutes later. At first, she did not cry or make a sound. I was screaming her name and praying for her to breathe. After what seemed like forever, she started making little sounds that worked up to an angry cry. I collapsed with relief. She was early, but she was healthy. Byron flew home that next weekend to meet his baby girl, Jessica. After Jessica's 8-week checkup, she was cleared for air travel. The kids and I packed up and flew to Colorado to reunite with Byron. This was another exciting day and another new beginning. We discovered a great little town south of Denver. It was the perfect place to raise our family. We lived in an apartment for a year while our new house was being built. We settled in, I got involved with the kids school, discovered we had great neighbors. Life was good again. I hoped that our struggles were over because we had been through enough.

There was one more challenge we had to get through first. Byron's job required a high-level security clearance. After 18 months of investigation and medical boards, it became terrifyingly obvious that he might not gain his clearance because of his illness. It had been three and a half years since his diagnosis with no subsequent episodes. All of his counseling sessions were positive and normal. The fact that he was on mental illness medications gave cause to the security clearance decision makers.

Byron was not able to perform the duties he was hired for until he gained his clearance. He had been give remedial duties to keep him busy. Byron sought out and created work for himself. This work had meaning and he was recognized for taking initiative. Byron was a liability on the company's overhead, but his immediate superiors fought for him, buying him precious time. Finally, there was nothing to be done. December 22, 1997 would be Byron's last day of work if his clearance wasn't approved. At that point, all we could do was to wait. I was at home around mid-day. I was keeping busy in the kitchen trying to ignore how bad I felt because I had a bad cold. The telephone rang. I answered. It was Byron. I couldn't believe my ears as he told me his clearance had just been approved! I dropped the phone and started screaming and jumping around like a fool. I had to laugh because there was no sound. My cold had stolen my "screaming level" voice. I picked the phone back up and heard Byron laughing. We both couldn't believe it. There was only two days left until the deadline.

We are still in Colorado. Byron and I will be empty nesters next summer. We are having a hard time wrapping our heads around that. We are all healthy and happy.

Our future looks promising after 25 years of marriage. We do not take anything for granted. The year 1994 and the few following years were scary. Our marriage and our courage were shaken to the foundation. We didn't know how things were going to turn out. We found strength in each other when we didn't know there was any left. We have earned the right to keep our promise made so many years ago. We will grow old together. Life is good.

Donna - Springfield, MO

I am Donna. I was voted one of the *Springfield Business Journal's 20 Most Influential Women of 2010*. I was 52 at the time. In the four years since the award, I have become more heavily involved in my local CASA chapter. I've been with my current CASA child for almost four years. She was 13 when she came into the foster care system and just celebrated her 17th birthday. What a journey we've been on! I've also starting teaching one day a week at our local community college. I teach classes on Resume' Writing and Interview skills. I am privileged to have the opportunity to influence the future through influencing young people. My sailor is an Ensign and the Electrical Officer on the USS Ashland which is home ported in Sasebo, Japan. After much soul-searching, I reached

the conclusion that I must be able to say the following things:
1. I was a good Christian
2. I was a good wife.
3. I was a good mother.
4. I was a good friend.
5. I made a difference in someone's life.

In order to pursue my life goals, I have purposefully not pursued a high-powered, high-profile career even though once I transitioned to public speaking; I certainly could have done so successfully. I have never regretted my decision, not even for a second. Though some will never understand my choice, I know that I traded misery for happiness, proficiency for passion, and frustration for fulfillment. What a deal!

My proudest accomplishment to date is having raised and influenced two daughters who will, in turn, become women of influence. My oldest, Kathy, is a recent graduate from MSU's Speech Language Pathology program. Kathy fervently desires to serve the deaf and hard of hearing community as well as children with autism. My youngest daughter, Sarah, is a Midshipman in the University of Missouri's NROTC program. While their paths are quite different, both of my daughters are using their unique gifts, talents and abilities to serve, to make a difference—one day at a time, one life at a time—just as I have taught them and modeled before them. As they grow and mature, so will their ability to influence. I could not be prouder!

Mentoring is my passion. In addition to personally participating, I try to transfer my passion whenever the opportunity presents itself. I have started several mentoring ministries in my local church and delivered seminars on mentoring to a variety of audiences in both the Christian and business arenas. Each of us has the power to change our part of the world." I've never aspired to change the whole world. I just want to positively influence my little corner of the world.

Jayne - Tyler, Texas

My name is Jayne and I married my high school sweetheart 27 years ago! Along with that, I gained custody of a stepdaughter from my husband's prior marriage. We both have two children together, a daughter 24 and son who is 21. My stepdaughter had a baby out of wedlock at age 17 and they both lived with us for a while. When I decided to move to Texas, my stepdaughter did not and stayed in CA to raise the baby herself. I decided to take the trip back to CA to see both my stepdaughter and grandbaby. When I arrived at their doorsteps, it was shocking to find out that my stepdaughter was on serious drugs. She was very pale, thin and eyes sunk in. I brought my four-year-old granddaughter home to Texas with me to raise. Eight months later, my stepdaughter came to Texas with her boyfriend. She was apparently clean and sober and got a job at a local deli. In the midst of this, our friend, and manager of the deli had a little daughter named Becky. Becky would frequent our home – and on several occasions would act very strange for a toddler. She would do things like take off all of her clothes, play doctor in the bushes and take off her underpants. The next thing we knew, our friends, Becky's parents, claimed my husband had violated Becky. My husband was prosecuted from the accusation of a sexual assault on Becky. The attorney fees and proceedings cost well over $65,000.

In May 2004, my husband was sentenced to LIFE IN PRISON. I was shocked and dismayed. My two kids were shunned. I was shunned by our church, and my friends were no longer social to me. I had no skills as my husband had earned a very good salary, and while I homeschooled my kids, financially I did not need to work at the time. Things had now changed dramatically for me – I needed to figure out what to do and get a job. I got a job at a local church being familiar with specific church software.

Since I was working at a low paying job, I lost my home, car, respect - the only thing left was my children. Both of my kids were forced to help support the household. As young as 15, they needed to work after school. I felt a sense of entitlement – after all this wasn't my mess – it was my husbands! I left the church job and took a job at a rural sanitation company. I wasn't myself and embezzled money from these wonderful people. Although I paid back what I took, they fired me - I couldn't blame them. I then found work at a local TV affiliate, but that barely paid the bills.

My son and I shared a very small apartment and while my boy was an Olympic hopeful, he received a full boat scholarship from a university in Texas. He went on with his first year and I moved back to CA. More bad luck happened when my son got caught drinking on campus and was thrown out. At that point, he chose to not return. He then had heard from another recruiter with an offer for a full scholarship to a college in Colorado. He did not accept it. My son decided to join the

U.S. Navy and he is currently serving proud!

It has been ten years since the awful incident in my life – I am healing and look to the grace of God that I am doing better each and everyday.

Gina - Morgan Hill, CA

This is a brief story of me as a mother!

I have four kids, ages 22, 19, 18 and 11. When the older kids were younger, I worked as a Compliance Manager for Restate in California and my husband was/is an Aircraft Mechanic. I made excellent money, actually more than my husband did; however, the kids had to go to an afterschool care, which was on site of their private Christian school in town. During the week was tough because they all had activities to attend to: karate, baseball, softball, art classes, swimming, homework, dinner, shower and bed on time. I commuted 20 miles to and from work, which equates to one-hour traffic time. Stressful week, every week, but weekends were family time.

I became pregnant with our younger child and we decided that I would not return to work and stay home with the kids. Of course, everyone loved this idea and I did too! Being a Compliance Manager in Silicon Valley Restate is very stressful and I felt guilty for how busy I was for work and that my kids were at school for so long, but of course, we enjoyed the income. My hubby and I made sure that everyone knew there were going to be changes for me staying home because our income would be cut more than half, but it was embraced. The kids had to transfer schools, which was not a big deal because it was in the same town.

I quickly learned to sew because it was much cheaper to make and repair clothes than to buy. I would buy clothes at Goodwill and the Salvation Army, change them little and embellish and no one was any wiser! I couldn't afford disposable diapers, baby wipes, formula or baby food. I made cloth diapers, used washcloths, breast-fed, pump milk, and made my own baby food with what we had. I did this not because I was environmentally conscience or into organic-natural stuff, it was because we could NOT afford this. Lucky for us we live in a town that has many farmers and they always have great deals on their crops. I wanted to apply for food stamps, but my husband refused so we never did. He worked lots of overtime whenever he could, always had side jobs, but was always home for dinner and Sundays was family day.

I made homemade breads, tortillas, etc. The kids loved it. Our friends were always commenting about how well I feed my family, always homemade foods, never store bought, hardly ever take-out -I just smiled, none of them knew that it was because we could not afford otherwise! We had $70 a week for food for a family of six. There were weeks when there was more, and some not. Everyone had a full tummy and hubby always had a good lunch! Birthdays and Christmas were also stressful, but the kids never knew.

My kids loved me being home, I was always in their classroom. I would volunteer (work) at the local Little League Baseball, so the boys could play during the season, same thing for the fast pitch league for our girl. Hubby would act as a maintenance manger at a local dojo so we could get a discount on all three kids' karate lessons. (They all have black belts by the way)

As the baby got older, I began to worry about preschool because I knew we could not afford it and I feel children needs preschool. A teacher told me that the local community college has an excellent preschool and it is income based and free for full time students. I always wanted a college degree but was never able to get one. I spoke with the hubby and he wanted me enroll right away! When I announced to the kids that I was going back to school full time, all the kids were excited except my oldest- his comment, "What about me!" He was a freshman in high school. I loved it, he still wanted me around! I wanted to work with Special Education and I began my college career! My then four year old was enrolled at an excellent preschool at the same school where I was.

Going to school full time has been difficult, but it greatly paid off. I have graduated and currently enrolled in a credential program and working on my Masters. I had three in high school at once one time and all of us always did out homework together! I have been working for the last four years as a Paraprofessional at the local school district. Over the years, the hubby has increased his income also. The first four years of our youngest life were extremely difficult on us. We just plugged along and it worked out great.

Brenda - Ames, IO

I thought you might like to hear about my grandmother. Her name was Ruth, and she was in her 50s in the 1970s when she went back to college. She started teaching before it was required to have a college degree, but in order to up her pension, she need to obtain a Bachelor's degree. When she went back to school, she was ahead of the "older" student movement. She was required to take Physical Education classes. A woman with crippling arthritis and a fear of water not only got a degree; she finished a swimming class with the grade of A+. She was my inspiration and I miss her so very much.

Janet - Tilton, NH

My name is Janet. I am a successful business owner in New Hampshire. I have been married two times and divorced that same amount! I just turned 50 and my life is amazing! I find it totally refreshing that I can find comfort in the small things in life and feel beautiful in my own body. I felt tied down and trapped in each of my marriages. I now feel free and know that my body is something I own and cherish. I feel sexy and more beautiful than when I was 20. Sometimes I really don't even care what people say or think. I live life to its fullest everyday and never take one day for granted!

Judy - Syracuse, UT

I started college when I was an 18-year-old newly married Navy wife. During my second semester of college, when my husband was on his first sea duty tour, I caught the flu and missed over a week of school. None in my family had ever graduated from college, so no one was pushing me to go to school, so, I didn't go back. After my husband's three years of sea duty, we had our first child and I became a stay-at-home mom. We made the tough choices to drive old cars and have hand-me down furniture so that I could stay at home. When my daughter was two, my husband got out of the military, and we began a series of moves across the country as he followed military contract jobs that lasted a year or two each. When my youngest daughter was in first grade, my husband's contract job ended again. After many discussions, I decided to go back to school to earn my degree, and my husband got a part time job where he could be at home in the afternoon and evenings when our children got home from school. I took classes when they were in school.

Going back to school in my late 30s was both challenging and exciting. I started out taking classes part time, because finances were tight. I spent many a night sitting at the table with my children doing my homework right beside them as they did theirs. There were many challenges in the next years that made me want to drop out of college again. The time that I was most tempted to drop out came just after Columbine when a student brought a gun to my oldest daughter's school. During the standoff, he shot the ceiling. When everyone was safe, my daughter was allowed to page me. I called the school and was told that there was a shooting at the school, and I needed to come get my daughter. I drove the 45 minutes home in terror. The students were afraid to go back to school the next day, and I was afraid to go to my class in case any of my children needed me. However, my kids encouraged me to go to school the next day.. It took a little more than five years, but just before I turned 40, I graduated **Summa Cum Laude** with a Bachelor's in English and Geography teaching. One fun fact is that I graduated with my college degree the same year that my oldest daughter graduated from high school.

Because I was worried that if I did not keep going to school, I would never go back, I applied to get a Master's degree. In Utah, you cannot start a Master's degree in English Teaching until you have taught for over a year, so I applied for a Master's in Educational counseling degree. Because I choose to teach in junior high, it turned out that earning the degree in Counseling was a blessing. I am able to use many of the lessons I learned in the counseling classes to help students every day. I graduated with a Master's in Educational counseling when I was 42.

I started my Doctorate degree the following month. I chose the school because it offered a degree in Educational Leadership with a minor in reading. There were many challenges within the time that I was in school for my advanced degrees, but I knew my children were watching my choices and I did not want them to see me fail. The biggest challenge happened in the middle of my Doctorate degree after my husband asked if I was okay with him going back into the military. For the next year and a half, my husband was gone for four to six months at a time as he completed the schools that the Army Reserve required for him to come back in. During one of those schools, I had to have emergency surgery. Because it was an online school, I got to attend classes by watching videos in my living room, so my son and daughter got to attend classes with me. They could have chosen to go into the other room, but they often chose to listen and watch my lessons. I graduated with my Doctor's degree in Educational Leadership when I was 48.

I do not really think that earning three degrees between the ages of 39 and 48 is especially amazing as anyone can do that. What I think is amazing is that I somehow managed to raise three amazing children while earning those degrees. My oldest daughter is a teacher with her Master's degree. My son is an Army medic. My youngest daughter will graduate from college next semester and is in the Navy reserves. THEY are my real amazing accomplishment.

Nikki - Shepherd, MI

Hey Laura,

Here is my story. I was in middle school when this guy in my neighborhood caught my eye. He was in high school and I was so flattered that he was paying attention to me. I thought that he thought I was "mature" enough to talk to. What I didn't know or understand at the time was what he wanted. I went to his house to meet for a walk. He invited me in for a bit, as he had some chores to finish. While I waited, we chatted about all the things girls and guys were interested in at that age. When he went to kiss me, I was scared and excited. Like any girl just in her teens, I was just amazed that he liked and was interested in me. When I got scared and tried to leave he wouldn't let me, instead, he chose to rape me. I don't know why he stopped mid way though but he did. Later when he called me, I confronted him on what he did, granted it was by the phone but that was safe, he couldn't hurt me. He threatened my family and me. For years, I let what happened rule my life. I just didn't know or understand it, because I knew it wasn't my fault. Through the years, I never told anyone but my best friend. I was broken without knowing how to fix it. Over the years through high school, I was hard shelled but I still romanticized what a relationship should be. The one guy who loved me for me, I broke up with. My fantasy for a "true love" relationship, he was to fly on a plane, swoop in, defy his parents, and declare his love. That didn't happen. Part of my brokenness. I eloped with my then husband, we had our daughter and divorced by the time she was three.

My husband, who was in the Army, spent money as if it was water. I had to find work that could bring in more income. I started working in a strip club as a server and eventually became a dancer. I worked as a dancer in three states before finally deciding to quit and lead a "normal" life. In walked a new guy. I was his mistress for about four years. I took the lie of him leaving his wife and wanting to be with me hook like and sinker. Four years of helping him run drugs, being his mistress, and his trophy that he paraded out like a toy. Four years of his abusive words, manipulations, lies and broken promises. The end came when I was court ordered into counseling for anger management after a domestic violence incident.

Almost three years of counseling for rape and abuse, I was finally about to break it off. The break up didn't come without a cost. I let my ex raise our daughter for her safety as I was being stalked and harassed. It seemed know matter how I tried to get my feet under me it wasn't happening. Finally, I didn't have a choice but to call the DEA after he threatened to have me killed. The next day, he went to visit my ex-husband and daughter. While I was in my counseling, I finally got the courage to heal by telling my parents of the rape when I was younger and the mess I was in. It still took years of a few more disastrous relationships, the last one before my now husband, that ended in an abortion. The abortion was my rock bottom. I had turned my back on all that I believed in. Shame is a powerful thing, it eats at you and tells you, that you are not worthy of anything or anyone. One year after the abortion, I got pregnant with my youngest daughter. The following year her father and I married. Two months after that I gained my life back. I accepted the gift of salvation of my Lord Jesus Christ. He made me a new creature. God has worked in my life on forgiveness, even the two men I never thought I could ever forgive, my rapist and the guy who was abusive. Forgiving them has allowed me to see them through Christ eyes and to allow Christ to work in my life fully. I now work on being a godly wife, and mom to my husband and four kids. By God's grace, I got out of the exotic dancer profession and I am currently drug and alcohol free. I know God was with me every single step, through every tear, heartache, struggle and joyful moments in my life. Thank you for reading and my prayer is that this story helps just one person walk out of the darkness.

Michelle - Carriere, MS

At the age of 47, and 25 years after I "started college", I finally obtained my Bachelor's degree in Management of

Human Resources from Faulkner University in Montgomery, AL. With that degree, I was able to transfer to NASA and finished out my 34-year civil service career working for the number one Federal Agency in government. Although I was not an astronaut, my job as a small business specialist was to help small businesses obtain government contracts with NASA. In 2011, my Center, John C. Stennis Space Center, won the Small Business Administrator's Cup that was presented to the Center having the overall best small business program. NASA's Administrator came down from Washington to Stennis and presented us with the "Cup".

Laura- San Antonio, TX

My name is Laura. I am 44 years old, a single mother of two sons, 16 and 19. I was born and raised in San Antonio, Texas and still live there today. My story is a complicated one. I come from a military family, my father being a highly decorated officer, raised to be perfect in every sense of the word. However, we were far from perfect. My father's alcoholism, abuse and the pressure of always having to appear perfect to others took a toll on my life from a young age. By the time I was 13, just after my parents divorced, I was drinking uncontrollably and using anything I could do simply stop feeling the pain. I tried very hard to seem perfect on the outside, but I don't really believe I was fooling anyone. By the time I was 18, I was sent to a treatment center for alcohol and drugs. I stayed two days. This wasn't for me. Instead, I moved from one friend's house to another until even they got tired of me.

By 23, I was living on the streets, smoking crack cocaine, doing whatever I needed to get it, and weighed in at about 68 pounds. I was dying. I was doing things that no well-brought up girl should do. That no girl should do- EVER. My family did an intervention on me. I ended up in a halfway house and I was separated from the drugs for good. That was January 11, 1993. When I got out of the halfway house, I had a job and a one-room apartment. That is when I believed that alcohol was never really my problem. I began drinking again after about nine months sober, and was off to the races once more.

One day I ran into my high school love's best friend. He told me he loved me and we got married and pregnant immediately. I thought this would be my cure. For the next eight years, I drank myself into oblivion.

We had had another son and I brought my kids into my disease. In 2002, I got sober again when my boys were four and six, and then divorced my husband. Soon after that I was married again, to a man who was sober. I thought this was the answer! Everything would be fine at last! This began 19 months of daily physical abuse. I was beaten down to nothing, and again I had brought my kids into a situation no kid deserved to be in. In 2004, I escaped one day, grabbed my boys and left with nothing. Another starting over, another school, another home. I began going to college and made the National Dean's List. I graduated with a Bachelor of Science in Nursing. I didn't know I was never going to be an RN. I had met someone else, a new guy who would fix it all and we married in 2007. Another beginning for my boys and me. Soon after I found this time and myself picking up a drink again- I stayed drunk, every day, all day. When they were little, my boys took care of me when I was drunk. This time they were just embarrassed. I was someone they were ashamed of once more.

Their father never came back into the picture and I was all they had. My husband was absent out drinking while I drank at home alone. The marriage ended with me having a couple of black eyes and him in jail. I had just turned 40. I was beaten by booze once more, and the awful realization that I had been looking for everything to make me a real human being in someone else. This time it was different, I was unemployed with one son in high school and the other in middle school. I was living on my brother's couch.

My mother and stepfather, who for twelve years had always let me work part time for them answering phones, asked me to come in while they were on vacation and cover the office. Six weeks later, they came back. I had made enough money to get us a little apartment and I liked what I was doing. I had started learning about commercial real estate twelve years earlier, and had my license. I begged them to teach me more. They acquiesced and gave me a full time job. I didn't know that this was going to be my future. I wanted to do everything I could to learn the ins and outs of the business. I started going to networking functions and brokering sales. My folks offered me a salary in lieu of commissions- so even if I wasn't making as much money as my colleagues, I had enough to feed my children. Then I got sick. They found 11 tumors in my neck on my thyroid gland and it had to come out. So did my entire reproductive system. I had always had thyroid issues but this was big. I had the surgery. I almost died after from an electrolyte imbalance. My mom covered the office for me while I was recovering, and I had a job to come back to. I didn't go back. I had found another husband to fix me!! - another mistake- another starting over for my kids and for me. It lasted nine months and I was divorced once more, for the fourth time. This was enough. This is when I began to work on myself. The only common denominator in all four marriages was me. What was I going to do about me?

I began therapy, stayed sober through a 12-step program and really uncovered some truths about myself. This was time consuming but worth it in every respect. I had finally regained the respect of my sons and the approval of my family. I still hated myself. In the last few years since I turned 40, the things that have happened have been amazing to say the least.

During the hard times, the broke times, the sick times, and the starting over times, my relationship with my sons grew into something I never thought possible. I went back to school for a Bachelor's in Business Administration. I learned more about the commercial real estate business and moved up to be the President of the company. I recently bought my first house. I bought the house next door to my mom and stepfather so I can be helpful to them. I have grown into someone who doesn't need others to validate her. I am happily single and fulfilled with a career and a path. I am a proud Navy mom who hates to see her son leave, but I know he is working for a bigger purpose. I work with and speak to groups of struggling alcoholics, sharing my story and my experience, strength and hope so they may find the freedom from the substances as I have found. When I was 23, I lived behind a shopping center. Today it is MY shopping center! I always thought my forties would be boring and dull – when you're young forty is way old, right? I have come into my own in the last four years. Later than most, but better late than never. I have lived unconventionally. Against the "norm", whatever that is. Today all that is the best part of me. I do not regret one second of my journey, and I look forward to the journey ahead. Today life is exciting and I could not be more grateful to be alive, healthy and happy.

Melissa - Philadelphia, PA

I am Melissa and I am 46 years old. I have been Assistant Scoutmaster to a Boy Scout troop of about 35 boys for the past four years. About a year and a half ago, we had the opportunity to sign up to do a 12-day backpacking trip at Philmont Scout Ranch in New Mexico. I jumped at the chance. After a year of training, taking practice hikes, figuring out which gear worked best, as well as joining a gym and losing 29 pounds, I set out on my adventure with two other adult leaders and seven boys. We actually went with a contingent of ten other troops from around Philadelphia - one hundred and six people total. I was the only woman. I encountered many different things along my trek that included a rattlesnake, buffalo, some elk and some long horned sheep. I also had to deal with an injury. On day seven, I injured my knee and I could not walk. I was taken off the trail by medical personnel and used crutches to get to the nearest staffed camp. It took 5 1/2 hours to reach the camp where a jeep was coming to pick me up and take me to the infirmary at base camp. I spent three days at base camp but was determined to get back on the trail.

On the fourth day, I got back on the trail and joined my crew. I was not starting out on this adventure and then not finishing it! While I was away, my husband was served divorce papers. I raised my two sons alone (one is a Ceremonial Guardsman in Washington DC, and one a high school student) without his help. I put up with verbal abuse for many, many years from him. At this point, I finally got the guts to divorce him. Being away, and hiking all that time showed me that I am capable of anything I set my mind to, to never ever give up, and to finish everything you start!!! It also reinforced to me the things that are important in life. Nothing - or no one can ever take this experience away from me. I learned a lot about myself in those 12 days.

Kate McKay - Newburyport, MA

This is a story of Kate McKay, LLC founded in 2012. Kate is known as the "Master Motivator". The company headquarter is in Newburyport, MA. Kate is a transformational speaker, coach, fitness guru, entrepreneur and mother of three whose passion is to spread her message of living a life of prosperity, health and abundance. She coaches and consults clients to propel themselves forward and live a full-on life. Aside from her newest book, "Living Sexy Fit", Kate has three e-books. Kate has a passion for fitness and inspires others to live their best life. In 2013, she competed in three National Fitness Bikini Competitions and placed in the top three of each show at the age of 50! Kate has inspired us all! She founded a multi-million dollar business called Gold Siena/Gold Party New

England, a precious metal dealer which partners with people to build their own businesses and celebrate prosperity, financial freedom and abundant living in both business and in all areas of life. Kate's newest book will be out soon.

Charlotte - Athens, TX

I've always tried to live my life by doing the right thing, so when my nine-year-old nephew wanted to come and stay a couple weeks one summer. I said, "Come on". How would I know that when he turned 20, he would join the U.S. Navy? See, he never left -he stayed with us.

That summer he convinced his mom to sign him over to us to live forever. Yes, we spent a year in counseling, to help him better understand why his mom cannot do the mom role and why he was living with us.

It wasn't always easy, most of the time we were scared to say the wrong thing, scared to be firm, scared to discipline-- and fearful that he would not understand and then run. He never did, he got mad, but he came around and understood that we were just looking out for his best interest. He had never been responsible for anything and never really had anybody that cared. Therefore, we gave him the chore of taking care of our dogs. He could not eat until they were fed, and he could not go to bed until they had fresh water. This was to show him responsibility and that he could care for others and in turn, others cared for him. He soon started telling his friends that we were his "mom and dad"- never really mentioning his real mom (my sister). I could not have stood by and watched him fall through the cracks, defaulter or fail and not become the young man that he has become today. He is my pride and joy. Just the thought of what he has become just brings me to tears. He is a handsome and strong young man that knows that we have his back 100 percent. When he came to stay with us, he asked for two things from me: 1) never forget him, and 2) never fail him. To this day, I have exceeded his expectations. It was really just about doing the right thing showing this young man that someone loved him, cared enough, and to be able to guide him to a wonderful life. So who would have known that one summer he would have gone from being my nine year old nephew without a purpose to the brave young man he is today-serving proudly as a United States Navy Sailor.

Susan - Johns Creek, GA

I am Susan and earned my Private Pilot's license at the age of 50. I had been a single mom for ten years prior and was in a rut. Therefore, I went out on a limb and did something I have always wanted to do for myself - learn to fly! It was a Godsend. It led to me meeting people who are now very important in my life, and to some adventures, I would not have previously dreamed of having.

These next few stories are a tribute to our United States Navy Sailors -

Karen - Kaneville, IL

I walked into our local Sam's Club today and a member of the Chicago Bulls was signing autographs so I got in line to get one for my youngest son. When Nazr Mohammed saw the shirt I was wearing "Proud Mom of a U.S. Sailor", he said, "Navy mom? Wow! That's pretty cool! "He then signed photos for our Sailor and my youngest son. I then told him thank you and he replied, "No ma'am, thank you!!" I believe I have a new respect for professional athletes in general.

Liz – Waterbury, CT

While standing at line in the post office, I asked the clerk about postage needed for a card that I was sending to someone on deployment. I was not certain if it was more than the usual cost of a postage stamp. The clerk asked if it was for my son, I replied "Yes". All the sudden a women way in the back of the line walked up to me and handed me a book of 10 stamps. She said, "Next time you write your soldier, the postage is on me." I replied, "OMG, thank you." She looked at me and said, "No, please thank him for his service." It took all I could do not to burst out crying right in the post office! There are so many kind people out there.

Karen - Kaneville, IL

My hubby was shopping at Trader Joes in Batavia, IL for some last minute things for our Sailor's pre-deployment party. The cashier asked him if he was having a party and he proceeded to tell her about our party. After he paid, she asked him to wait a minute and she proceeded to get my hubby a huge bunch of beautiful flowers for our party, on the house. That was not only classy of this woman, but also classy of Trader Joe's! This random act of kindness totally made my day!

Kathy – Cheyenne, WY

Nine years ago, I was pregnant with my first son and I gained 35lbs. I was 128 lbs. after I had my son, lost most of my weight, and I was pretty happy. I never really worked out, but I was active. Fast-forward four years, I had my second son and gained 30 lbs. This time it took longer to get rid of the weight, but I got down to about 135 lbs. About six months prior to my second birth, I ended up loosing my job and was a stay at home mom. There were some struggles with work for my hubby, we had to move to Montana for a while, and then after about five months, we moved in with my parents. I was depressed and did not like the way I looked at all. By the time my second son was a year old, I was up to about 145 lbs. and miserable. He was a tough baby and didn't sleep much. The combination of being sleep deprived and feeling the way I did about the way I looked was not helping. I was down on myself and I really didn't like anything about myself.

When my second son was about three, we moved to North Dakota for my hubby's job. We lived there for about seven months before I headed back to live with my parents. One day I was surfing the net and found a Face book page about a girl that did online training. I signed up for her online coaching and started to eat better and workout. All the workouts where done at home. I joined her in late February and by July; I was looking and feeling so good. I had lost almost 20 lbs. At this point, I felt like I wanted to do more.

In December of 2012, I decided to shoot for my first Bikini competition and joined Body Ambition... In June of 2013, I did my first competition in Miami, FL. During my preparation, I shared progress on a Face book page. Many women inquired about the food, how it was prepared, and what kinds of things I did for workouts. I wanted more so I decided that I would help other moms and woman realize that setting a goal can do so much for you. I plan to do more competitions as well as work toward achieving my Personal Trainer Certification. I have a cookbook in the works and I already have a workout guide that I created. You saw what I could do – you can do it too!

Doreen - South Elgin, IL

I graduated from Northern Illinois University with a degree in Accounting in May 1989. I was married a month later. My son was born in July 1991 and my twin daughters were born in February 1995. I have worked in various accounting positions all these years. My latest position is the Business Controller - Financial Services at Sears Holdings Corporation. In 2009, I realized that my career wasn't going to go much further without a Master's degree and CPA designation. They positions that were open to advance required one or both of these things. I started to get my Master's degree when my twins were three. It was just too much to work full time, go to school and take care of the kids. In 2009, when I was 44, the kids were in high school so I thought it was the best time to go back to school. I finished my Master's degree in Accountancy in February 2011 from Keller Graduate School of Management. Concurrently, I studied for the CPA exam. I passed all four parts on the first attempt. I felt that that was a terrific accomplishment because not everyone can do that. This education has helped me so much in my accounting career. With the large raise, I can now put my daughters through college. They will now surpass all the accomplishments I have had.. I am hoping I provided inspiration showing that one can go back to school no matter what age.

Virginia - Garland, TX

Sometimes when I look back, I am amazed at what I have accomplished. First a little about me, I am a twin. My mom's first husband died and left her with four boys. She met my Dad who was younger than she was. Daddy married her and wanted two more kids. Mom said that because she was going to turn 40 soon, and she already has four kids, they would need to settle on just one. Surprise to both, she had twins and I was twin B. I joined the Navy while still in High School at 17. I lied to my Mom to get her sign the papers telling her that I would become a Nurse. The truth was I joined to become a Corpsman. Recently, when my son called from boot camp crying how hard it was I had to laugh. "Gee kid, Mama did it, and I now you can too". He is now a Corpsman like me. I left active duty when pregnant with my first son. They wanted to send me to the Philippines so I asked for a discharge and moved to Dallas to be with my husband. I did go into the reserves after I had my first and retired in 2000 with nine years active and 12 reserves. During my life's adventures, I managed to drill, go back to school to become an RN, and have four kids.

Carissa - Appleton, WI

I have three boys. I have worked full-time as a Marketing Research Manager since the youngest was born. This means that I travel about 20-25% of the time for work. I have a spouse that has been in restaurant management for the same amount of time. For the most part, my life has always been challenging, so I don't think much about it. I wanted to share the 18 months or so that turned out to be the most challenging of my life.

As I look back on my life, one date stands out to me as being the start of that year – September 11, 2001. I know that we share the grief that day means to our country. It was the personal events that day that triggered the upcoming time so stressful. My boys were 13, 10 and 7 at the time – so they had mixed levels of comprehension of those day's events- My dad worked in aviation as an airframe & power plant technician/aircraft inspector. On September 11, we were living in Bradenton, FL. Our experience on 9/11 was the same as everyone else's – sheer disbelief and utmost grief.

Things changed the next day. I was at work, and my husband called to ask me if my dad worked for the high profile - Venice, Florida based flight school. I recognized the name of his new employer (he had been there several months) and my husband told me the FBI had seized the building and were questioning employees. I quickly called my dad and he contacted the local field office in Michigan. He was asked to present himself immediately, and was questioned about terrorists. The **SAME** terrorists that flew into the Towers had trained at this particular Florida flight school!

Dad called me that night, relieved that he had not met any of them. Things changed on that Friday when he called me again –his voice quivered indicating how upset he was. As it turned out, one of the terrorists that had flown into the World Trade Center had confronted him. Dad had grounded the training plane for maintenance and wouldn't release it until it was airworthy. Clearly, he had been haunted by the interaction and things got bad at work. Clients stopped using the well-known Florida flight school blaming them for the terror attacks. My dad and his co-workers had to race to the bank to cash their paychecks each week in fear of the checks bouncing... This stress probably caused my dad to miss some very important health cues.

He could no longer hide the headaches and all of the confusion he was experiencing – because it cost him his job. When he finally confided that he had been having ongoing headaches, I talked him into going to the doctor. The next several months were a blur, and I can barely remember any of the days. There were two months of daily radiation treatment. Dad moved in with us, as he was no longer able to care for himself – although he didn't understand why. I continued to work full time and took care of the kids and my dad. I was literally taking life an hour at a time, because that's all I could handle.

Dad spent eight weeks in hospice care. We watched him slip away slowly – first forgetting family members, then losing his connection to reality. One afternoon, after a visit from my middle son, he fell asleep and didn't wake again. About two weeks later, he passed.

I have carried a lot of guilt from that time because near the end, I had been praying for him to pass so the suffering would end. When he passed, I had no idea how "final" his death would be, or how guilty I would feel. It has taken 11 years, but I have finally let go of most of the guilt. I still don't know how I made it through this time but I did.

Ann - Suffern, NY

My name is Ann and I would love to share my story with you. In 2006, I started building a dollhouse for myself as a hobby. When it was finished, I really had nowhere to keep it so I decided to sell it on EBay. The house and furnishings cost over 300 dollars yet it only sold for 100. My daughter who was interning at Hackensack University Hospital at the time told me I should have donated it to the kids going through chemo there. We had another one in the house so that is what I did. It was a hit with the kids and so I had the idea that since I enjoyed building them I would donate more and the doctors could give them to the kids as a gift from them, not me. I thought it would be better coming from them than from a stranger especially with what they would be facing with these doctors.

Since then, I have built and donated 340 dollhouses. When I first started, all the houses went to Hackensack Hospital in New Jersey. My daughter would deliver them to the doctors. After graduation from Duke, she applied to Yale for graduate school. From that point, all the houses went to children at Yale. During these years, I also donated every Christmas to my local Police Department for children in need. The police chief here hand picks the kids that were literally getting very little and let Santa bring them a dollhouse. I usually try to have at least ten built for this program every year. I started a face book page called Dollhouses for Kids Battling Cancer a few years ago and then things really took off. I am not a non-profit, so I do not accept cash from anyone. People however wanted to help so they would send me items they no longer wished to keep such as bedroom sets, kitchen, living room, etc. They sent wallpaper, dolls and fabrics. Three dollhouse companies got involved. The Magical Dollhouse Company started helping me almost from the very beginning by setting up a donation page. People go to that page and select a dollhouse that they pay for and the company sends it to me to build and donate to a child. The Greenleaf Dollhouse Company heard about them and they offered to pay shipping on any house purchased for me from the Magical Dollhouse Company so the customer is not charged. HBS/Miniatures. com set up a program where people buy gift cards for me, they hold them and when I need something I order it and it is sent to me for free. I honestly don't know where I would be without all of this help. When I started, I paid for everything myself; houses, furniture, dolls, etc. Now I pay for a few dollhouses, paint, glue, furniture and dolls here and there.

Since starting the Face book page I got a lot of exposure that has given me so much of the help I spoke of, but it also got me many requests for dollhouses for children that live quite a distance from me in NY. Shipping became out of the question when the costs of some was over 150.00. I just could not afford it. People offered to pay the shipping costs but again, I am not a non-profit so it would be illegal to accept cash donations. I do not want to become a non-profit because this was, and never will be, about money. One day I had a request for a dollhouse for a child in Rochester, NY. I really hate saying

saying no, so I had an idea to ask if anyone on my Facebook page living in my area that might be headed that way in the near future. Within a few hours, people started responding that they wanted to help. The whole thing was set up and the child got her dollhouse within a week. After that I figured why not shoot for the stars. When I get a request, no matter where it is, I just ask on my Face book page, and every single time it has worked out. Dollhouses have been delivered to 21 states and even to Canada. One woman packed her sister and all their kids in the car, drove from her home in Michigan to my home in NY to pick up a dollhouse, drove it to Canada to a little girl, and then drove home to Michigan!

I now have 105 Dollhouse Delivery Angels from 37 States willing to drive dollhouses to children with cancer. The average miles these angels have driven is 489.

Every time I have posted a request for drivers, my delivery angels always answer! I have never been stuck and never been turned down. Personally, I like to think that God has His hand in this and that He is happy with what we are doing because it works out every single time, with out fail and that is amazing. Therefore, that is my story.

Jeannie - Sheridan, OR

I love the concept of your project! I would love to share my story of being a teen mom at age 16, and overcoming every horrible statistic that was against me. By the grace of God, I graduated, married the baby daddy, and had two more children. I now have a 22-year-old married daughter who gave birth to the world's sweetest baby last Thanksgiving. My 19-year-old son is in the Navy, and my 16-year-old daughter is college bound with a solid 4.0 GPA. I sound like I am bragging, but I am so amazed at what a beautiful life I have. Nothing fancy, but tons and tons of beauty in it. My purpose is to acknowledge and celebrate every good and perfect thing that comes my way. I now volunteer at my daughter's high school by teaching teen moms how to cook and show them encouragement.

Denise – Everett, WA

I truly believe sharing this helps more people out of the dark and we all need to know that we are not alone. Thanks for letting me share my story. I was born and adopted in 1966 in Redding, CA. I had a dad, mom, older sister and older brother. We were an upcoming middle class home and by the time I was 11 we were very middle class level. There was always food, clothes, warmth, and we never wanted for anything material.

That was the outside looking in. I grew up with my dad very sick. He has diabetes and hardly checked his blood sugar more than once a day, so he was not very healthy for most of my life.

He began dialysis when I was about eight. By the time I was 12, he was going downhill quickly - he needed a new kidney, suffered three heart attacks and had two amputations. He passed away when I was 13 and it was a blessing. He had been an abusive husband and more than once I had witnessed him throwing my brother across the room and he had hit my sister a few times. He used to beat the daylights out of my mom about once every two-three months. He was a clever guy though and never left a mark for the rest of the world to see- only the torso, under the hair or high enough on her arms.

I was not sad to see him go, nor was my mom. I think she would have eventually divorced him but he got sick too fast she decided why bother. My brother was the real piece of work in the family. He was continually in trouble for something minor, but a star high school football player, decent grades, and popular. No one had a clue what a monster he was. My brother abused me from before I can remember until I was 12. We don't know when it started but the wise counselor who finally diagnosed me with PTSD when I was 31. I had had my first flash back then and was actually considering suicide. That counselor, Randy -changed my life.

I had attempted suicide three times as a young teen, and knew the signals. I was well aware that I needed help. I was a chronic runaway; I smoked lot of marijuana, smoked cigarettes, and drank my fair share all before 14. I hated school, and likely spent one day a week skipping and stole my mom's Valium a few times as well. It all came to a head when I was 14 and ran away again after a friend stole my mom wedding rings. After weeks couch surfing, I was picked up with a group of kids 16-21 years old. We were in possession of firearms in a state park so off I went to juvenile hall. Since I had broken no law, my mom said, "Take her away, I am sick of her" to a counselor at a shelter in Seattle for teen runaways and he took me there. I found encouragement to tell what had happened- one day before being let back on the street, I fessed up and everything changed. I went to a foster home for I think four days and my mom came to me and said I needed to come home- but only if I would press charges. I said, "Yes". Turns out my sister told mom she knew what was happening but was afraid of David so she didn't tell either.

They extradited my brother almost a year later from CA. He had found out police were watching and waiting for him to check his mail. We think an ex-girlfriend "spilled the beans", but he had threatened her life to. He had sexually abused and beat her- she was terrified.

When he finally got to Seattle he confessed but the statute of limitations was in his favor, and we ended up settling for one count child rape and two counts of indecent liberties (I hate that judge, I really do). He spent less than one year in prison. He spent more time in jail for breaking his parole than for the crimes he committed. As it turns out, I was only the first. Since he got out, he abused his girlfriends' two daughters and at least one child in Texas. The other girlfriend's uncle tried to kill him one night in a bar and spent five years in prison for attempted murder. That man is a hero to me. He has/had spent most of his time hopping borders between Costa Rica (loose extradition laws), CA, and TX. We had one report he was dead but I have searched and do not see a death record anywhere. I still live on alert in fear but have learned as well that I am alive because of this (hyper- vigilance). I am alive and kicking because I had a very strong role model, my amazing mother. I am alive because I KNEW God had another plan. I remember sitting on the porch on night with a couple bottles of pills when I was 13. I was crying and praying to God to let me know if I should stay because I didn't want to. I prayed a desperate prayer like I hadn't before or any since He answered by sending me a shooting star, the brightest one I've seen ever. I decided to stay and stopped thinking suicide was the answer. That is how I know the signs and know when to ask for help. That is one of the most important lessons I learned- when to ask for help.

My husband was a high school friend. A "Greek God" that I fell madly into puppy love with at first sight. We did not date until I was 23. We always partied together - I knew he was a heavy drinker. I did not know he came from a family that was as screwed up as mine - no sexual abuse, but tons of beatings and an addict step-dad. After 7-8 years of marriage, one amazing son, and one dismal miscarriage, it became bad - vicious at times. Words were weapons and any form of control was okay. One night it became physical - he threatened to kill me with a hammer to my head. I decided, "Fuck this I am done" and told him to kill me right now, but looked down under the table first. Hiding under the table was our 5-year-old hiding behind the Rottweiler. He dropped the hammer and left the house. The next day I told him I was taking Josh to the zoo. Instead, I went to court, got a restraining order and with mom's help, got the hell out of there.

I grew up in hell and so did Josh's dad. Josh would not. I promised God when he was born I would be a good mom and do right by him. He trusted me with this most precious and amazing gift of Josh and I would never put that child through what I went through. A vital part of this is that I have always had some faith in God. Not always very strong in it but has always been there. The moment Josh was born, that very second, something amazing happened. I was taken off the table (C-section) and appeared before God. It was just God and me in this amazing, beautiful, warm, and comforting place - I felt no fear, I knew God loved me and always had. I bowed before him and all around me was flames - like warm velvet, sort of like a puppy licking me all over even inside my soul. God told me, "I am giving him to you because I love you and I trust you but he is Mine". Since that day, I have had a new faith, an unwavering faith. No matter where my son goes as a Corpsman, I know that his Marines love him like their mama and I know God has his back. I know now that there really is more and that this world is to love on another. It is a contradiction to me that Josh would choose a warrior life, but I know what he stands for and what I taught him; Respect and Love and to stand up for someone who can't. You never know who is an angel. So, if you see a hungry person on the street give him a sandwich, you are saving yourself in that act of kindness and human respect. I still have times when I go off the deep end but recognize then know and have the tools to deal with them. I don't hide in my house anymore and fear the world anymore. I love the world and look for the small miracles that God shows us every day. I am truly a survivor, and victorious now. God and my son have shown me that.

Madelyn - Philadelphia, PA

This is a story of Madelyn who has worked at her father's Hispanic newspaper for the past 20 years. The paper was ready to close due to the economy a few years ago. Madelyn's father is 81 – a printer by trade started this newspaper in 1996. He started this as a part- time endeavor in the family basement. The first three years they made little money, but because of the passion and perseverance, they stuck with it. It has been a struggle for sure, as advertising is expensive and the internet has taken over. Madelyn and her dad have found a niche market because some readers coming from other countries appreciate the ability to pick up a paper and read it easily. The name of the newspaper is El Hispano Newspaper and the website is El-Hispano.com. This is a family run newspaper which survives because of Madelyn's' endurance and belief in her father's dream!

Carolyn -Tacoma, WA

I was a single mom and raised my daughter myself, from before 18 months of age. She was the product of a short and horrible marriage. She is 24 years old, graduated from Santa Clara University, and on her career path. My name is Carolyn. My entire life I wanted to be an artist. Then life happened and reality set in and I decided to become a Corrections Officer because I wanted to help people. All the while, I continued creating art. When I had my daughter, I went to the Art Institute of Seattle. I attended an accelerated course in the evenings since I worked all day. I was in a terrible and very short marriage at the time and sometimes even had to bring my baby to classes with me. I brought art into the correctional environment and even orchestrated an art show with the inmates. It was good to see the great pride they had in their works. In 1994, I became self-employed and became co-owner in a sign shop. Still having my two art shows per year that I had had in whatever home I was living in since the 7th grade. (My mom always knew how important art was). I left that sign shop in 1994, opened my own shop, and left my corrections job. Within two months, I was unable to walk due to a herniated disc. Early on, my work consisted of watercolors, charcoals and other paintings. My first great watercolor was designed at the age of five - a pair of wet tennis shoes. As time progressed, I realized my passion for jewelry - so I started to create jewelry. After a year, I added fused glass and painted glassware. When my brother passed away in 2008, I started Sacred Embers that is fused glass with the ashes of people and pets. THIS is the most amazing work that I do.

On September 1, 2012, I opened Creative Forces Gifts & Sundries located inside the Four Star, Hotel Murano in downtown Tacoma. This hotel has special meaning to me because we had a huge fundraiser for St. Anthony's Oncology Center in Gig Harbor, WA, in honor of my brother here. Someone that worked in the hotel knew of my work, approached me, and asked if I would be interested in having a shop in the space that was available. It all worked out, and because I had had the vision in high school of having a gallery someday to show my work, as well as promote other local artists- it seemed like a fairly easy process.

I truly feel that the stars aligned and there is the energy of my brother here. It will continue to grow and be more and more successful. I began the shop with the works of 12 artists and currently have 41 artists represented -100% local. It took me until I was 50 to do it, but I DID IT! Sure, it isn't where I want it yet but it is going in the right direction. I am very proud of the shop/gallery. To hear people say that my shop is probably the best gift shop they have ever seen in a hotel is wonderful! It is amazing to call an artist and tell them that a celebrity purchased their piece or it went to another country. It is all hard, long hours of work but I am loving my life and enjoying my accomplishments. I have won several awards for the shop and for myself via this platform.

Candace - Forked River, NJ

This story was submitted with permission from Candace Capone. I hope we can all learn by this story by putting an end to drug use in the United States. Portions of this story were originally published in the *Woodbridge Patch.com*. This story is about an amazing mom who has fought, and will continue to fight tirelessly by sharing the story of her son, Michael's addition. She encourages others to talk about addiction – something she was afraid to do while her son was still alive.

Michael, who would have turned 20 in August, died on a Tuesday of a heroin overdose after years of battling addiction. Candace fought hard as well, doing everything she could to try to get her son to quit. She didn't talk about it too much for fear she would face the brutality of the name-calling and hopeless stereotypes that are often hurled at parents like her. There's "scumbag," "white trash," and an endless supply of others, she said. Sadly, it is apparent that the name calling doesn't even stop after an addict is dead." "Every single family has the same exact story and nobody wants to admit it or talk about it because we are called 'scumbags'", she said.

I'm afraid to tell people because they think birds of a feather flock together." For Michael, it started with marijuana. Later he turned to oxycodone pills. Then came heroin. "It's only five dollars a bag," Candace said, cheaper than illicitly obtained prescription drugs. However, those who know addiction know the Capone family was, and is, like many others – a typical middle class family, until the rug had been swept out from under them.

Michael was a star wrestler who loved fishing and skateboarding. He did well in school and had plenty of friends and family members who loved him. Even after he was addicted to heroin and being sought by the police, people were able to see the kind person he was below the surface."The police found him and he was hungry after not eating for days," Candace said. "They said he was such a nice kid that they took him to lunch before arresting him. "Lacey police officers were always respectful, professional and helpful", Candace said. The prosecutor's office helped arrange to place Michael in rehab, but he escaped and fled for days before the police found him.

Heroin does not discriminate. It doesn't matter if you are male or female, short or tall, rich or poor, young or old. Once in your veins, the person who you always loved and cared for becomes a stranger. A beast in his own mind, whose only goal in life is to get the next fix…chasing the very first high that they have felt. "Scumbag!" Every article I have ever read about people being arrested for drugs always has comments made by their readers that say that word. I can assure you that they are sadly mistaken.

My son's name once lit up the newspapers of his glorious

days as a wrestler and as a little boy entering fishing contests. Now the papers print his name for his arrests from heroin addiction. My son was raised with love. A good boy he once was. Now all that remains is the addict he has become, willing to steal, lie and cheat his own family to get his next fix. My son loved wrestling. He was once an undefeated junior varsity team member. His room still boasts the trophies that he had won. He loved to fish and skateboard. Now all that remains are the photos of those happier days from that child who is now a man addicted to heroin. Am I bad mother? Is this my fault? Why are people blaming me? How do you tell your friends and family that one morning you went to wake your child for school only to find him not breathing, eyes rolled in the back of his head, and his body an eerie grey color that is unimaginable? How do you tell them that you frantically performed CPR on him, awaiting the ambulance, with tears streaming down my face while Michael almost dies in my arms? Imagine my horror, after my son was transported to the local hospital, I flip his mattress and find bags of heroin and a hypodermic needle. How did this happen to "MY SON"? My days and nights were filled with watching over him-protecting my home and younger son that lived with us. How do you go out and put on a happy face when your child is killing himself. How do you sleep when you fear your child may steal from you and sneak out as you sleep?

That very same morning, I wanted to flush away the heroin and protect my son. Would that be the right thing to do? I called his probation officer, crying and begging for help. He advised that he would make some calls on my behalf, but to turn everything over to the police. As advised, I drove to the police station, with heroin in my purse, a nauseous, sick feeling in my stomach, and turned my own son in. Two years have gone by since that day. Nothing has changed. I have spent countless hours and dollars trying to save his life. I always visited him at rehab and juvenile detention, bringing him clothing and toiletries. I showed my love and support. I remember one night I was told my son was down the street "using." I went there without hesitation, without thinking. I busted into the home and verbally lashed out at the dealer. My son went out through a window. How crazy am I to put my own safety on the line to save my son? How much does love and hope cost. I have spent my hard-earned money on fines, lawyers, co pays-you name it! I remember being a teenager and seeing a commercial from Carroll O'Connor saying, "Get between your kids and drugs any way you can." He wasn't acting. The look on his face said it all. Now as a mother myself, I get it. My son has passed, I hope quickly and painlessly. I WILL love him until the end of time. Now, when my friends and family ask what they can do to help me, I respond to them, "Get between your kids and drugs- any way you can." There are parts of this story that have been intentionally left out, as they are too hard to tell.

Mel – Tacoma, WA

Why do I like myself more after 40 than ever? During my period of low self-esteem and extreme uncertainty of being young, I relentlessly questioned every aspect of my life. I would often go to bed frustrated and upset as I asked myself 'why wasn't I good enough'. I decided to silence that voice inside of me and asked myself what would really make me happy. I have always been very creative and expressive so I choose to change that thinking. Oh, it took a LOT of work to de-program some of the thinking, but the other side is a beautiful place and I'm so grateful for the peace and forgiveness I've been able to find on this side of life. I have realized that I am content with myself and have become proud of who I am. I do not worry as I did when I was younger. I have realized that everything happens for a reason and that it all will fall into place. Staying up all night worrying about something isn't healthy for my spirit. I realized that trying to impress and pleasing everyone happiness comes from feeling content with your own life and goals. They say a talented adult is merely a child who survives. This holds true for me in many aspects. I have learned to embrace my talents and quirkiness. It's what makes me unique. It sets me apart and makes me amazing.

I love my talented, problem-solving mind. I surround myself with like-minded, positive people. I decided that I want to be that person who not only enjoys playing the game well, but also one who creates new ideas and invents new and hopefully better ways of being. I stopped having expectations and expecting others to understand my needs and expecting them all to live up to them. If I need something, then it's my job to explain that. No one-NO one is perfect.

I believe in my life path. I know that my life belongs to me and its okay to be focused on what I want. There have been people along the way who have tried to make me feel bad for my focused mind/goals. I realized that is about THEM, not me. Being focused and driven has caused me to work to live on a high understanding of life. I choose to live an enlightened life. I choose to get better every day. I choose to challenge myself and trust my decisions. I choose to be happy.

Sandra - Gilbert, AZ

I always felt my parents did not want me. Maybe I was a burden on them. That perhaps was not true. I do not know what made me do what I did, other than the fact I felt imprisoned and unable to voice my wants and needs to them. I ran away when I was 15 with a high school sweetheart - my first love. We drove to Nebraska in the middle of winter in his VW Bug that had a rusty floor with holes in it covered in ice. We ran out of money, so we headed back to Cedar Rapids where our parents awaited. His parents placed him in a psychiatric facility. Mine changed the locks and shortly thereafter moved to Phoenix, AZ. I have to say though that they did buy me a winter coat, gave me a few of my belongings, and asked if I would like to go with them. By then I was sixteen in another relationship and living with my boyfriend's parents. I continued schooling, and in my senior year, I got pregnant.

The principal at the time did not like that I was pregnant. She felt I was something she did not want in her school and that I might somehow lead someone else astray. Even though I had only four electives to complete with only a semester left she called me into her office one day and kicked me out of school. I was so angry at the time and felt the system wasn't looking out for me anyway so why should I fight it or go back to school elsewhere.

I was married when I was five months pregnant to my baby's dad. Once my baby was born, I saw that I needed to be able to provide for him more than working as a Nursing Assistant in a long-term care facility. I loved my job caring for the elderly. They all felt like I had this big family with many grandparents. I was very good at my job and knew my responsibilities. There were two nurses at this facility that influenced my decision to further my career and go into the Nursing program. I looked into what it would take to do this and felt the Adult High School Education program was the way to go since I felt I truly earned my diploma and felt a GED would lessen what I had accomplished in the first place. I don't recall how long this took me, but it wasn't long. This was also around the time certifications became mandatory for nursing assistants.

My husband at the time was laid off from employment for two years. I saw his behavior and self-esteem change. He became very jealous of anything I did including hanging out with my best friend. He became abusive while I was pregnant- physically and mentally. It would come in spurts, but when my son was two years old, I decided it was enough.

Upon leaving him, I was faced with being a single parent with no support from him. He eventually got a job, but rarely paid his support. I struggled for a bit and ended up changing jobs for higher pay and detailing cars. This is where I met the husband I am still married to. I finally decided to do what those two nurses told me I needed to do for my family and me. I went back to school. I had a ruptured ectopic pregnancy in 1992 while in the nursing program. I was told I should drop out for my body to be able to heal, but it wasn't guaranteed that I would be accepted into the next semester. I plunged ahead with staples in my belly and a lot of pain. I graduated the nursing program with an Associate's degree in 1993. My youngest was born in 1994 and struggles with Bipolar Disorder and Autism. I went back to school in 2001 and in 2003 received my BSN. I battled health and wellness but continue to rise above it. Maybe at a young age it was drilled in me to work hard at everything I do. I see myself as someone who has always fought to maintain control of my life and to prove others wrong. I have proven that anyone can rise above it. I believe it takes determination to succeed.

Dixie - Wasilla, AK

I was born and raised in Rawlins, Wyoming by my Dad and Aunt. I have one younger brother who now lives in OK. I graduated from high school in 1980 as a Science Geek. Originally, I was going to join the Navy or attend CSU but decided to pursue a degree in Engineering. The plan was to finish up at University of Wyoming, but after a year of college, I found out math was not my forte'. I decided that I would go into Environmental Science and eventually get into Engineering. Therefore, I left Wyoming, took off to Bozeman, MT to pursue my degree in Environmental Science, and graduated in 1985. I came home, dumped my all my belonging into a storage, and took off to Northampton, West Australia for an Exchange Program. I learned all about sheep and wheat farming, and being an American, this had positive/ negative connotation. I really missed home and my freedom.

No, I did not like Australian men (Blokes) for some are male chauvinists.

After a year, I returned home to look for work and a place to live. I frantically looked for work, but due to the economy and no actual experience, I was out of luck. So on June 17, 1987, I enlisted in the Navy. I had to wait for four months to go in, (I sat for days in, and crocheted an afghan since I was unemployed and was totally out of my element – 23 and had never lived in the area where my Aunt lived). On the 22 of Oct 1986, I shipped out to Orlando for booking and was released on the 24th of Dec, A day I will always remember for I was sick with pneumonia and I happened to lose my ID. I flew to Norfolk and when I reported in, they had no idea why I was there as everybody was gone for the holiday.

Eight month later after training to become an OTA (Ocean Systems Tech Analyst - Anti Sub Marine Warfare), I came home for three weeks on leave which is not recommended before I headed to Adak with the intention to be stationed for 15 month's .The next duty station would be Iceland - then the plan was to get out. Well, God had more in store than I had ever imaged. I met a NC born Sea Bee (wild one that eventually became a HA and after 22 years returned to NC and I remained in AK - a good thing) and the rest is history .While I was in Adak, AK I served four years and then Jim was born. At that point, I moved to Anchorage. From there, I moved back into my career and Garrett arrived in 1993 - life became challenging at all fronts. Then Mark joined the HA and I was told it my way or the highway, so I took the highway.

In 1995, life took a 360, as I lost the boys and had to pay child support. The games began. In the process, I learned how to be Paralegal, represented myself in court, lost my job and became an Insurance Agent for Prime America. I also worked as substitute teacher, facilitated a few other gigs in order to make the grocery money and a roof our heads, and learned how to become an advocate. This was all accomplished while raising the boys (mom, soccer mom, wrestling, the Chief, Cook and the bottle washer) and dealing with antics from their dad. No, it was not easy especially living and working in AK where it is quite cold and one must learn how to deal with winter for eight months/years. Never the less, I learned how to manage many tasks, and making the best of it, (I was mom and dad to two strong-willed boys who were taught that church, school and work are three things that are not options to overlook. Furthermore, you always need a plan and a back plan -if you have a dollar think before you spend. Lastly, the woman you marry will not be like (operate) like your Grandma Banner or me. In 2006, while I was in transition, not able to move within my career field, and being told my degree had expired, which I found frustrating, I decided to earn my Masters. That was a lot of fun/work. However, it was a well worth experience/investment. Weeks later, I sent Jim off to the USN and three years later sent Garrett off to the USN. Both are doing well, becoming strong, and loving good men. – No, it is not easy to cut the ties, but they do know right from wrong. The Ice Queen will always be there, but she will try her best to put in her two cents in, to remind them of the need for education and professionalism. Then, on Aug 12, I married my FedEx Man who I had dated for 9 years. I was married at 25 and it lasted 8 years and re- married at 50- so it was a WOW moment. We are starting a new business in Logistics.

He is the Ops and I facilitate the Admin while working in the oil and gas business so we can bring on the new AK LNG Pipe Line. Never a dull moment, and like I told my husband since we said, "I do", life has been a blur. My future goal is to be a Life Coach for women which would concentrate on life skills and financial planning. My other goal is to find a way to become a "Snow Bird" so I can migrate between the Lower 48, live, enjoy the United States, and be closer to my boys.

Julie - Port Ewen, NY

My first marriage only lasted 3 1/2 years. The marriage was an abusive relationship that I was lucky to get out of. My ex-husband was both an alcoholic and had drug problems. I had to depend on my parents to buy groceries and diapers for my son. We were on WIC so that I could get medical coverage and formula for my son. We never had money because when my ex- husband actually did work, he spent all the money on drugs. When my son was 11 months old, I left my husband and moved in with my parents.

I started nights at IBM working in manufacturing when my son was one year old and, stayed on night shift until he was six. I started going to the local community college when he went to preschool. I eventually I got to days when my son went into first grade. I got a promotion into a finance job at IBM. I continued working and going to school for the next six years. When I graduated from Marist college with my MBA, my son was almost 16 years old. I stayed at IBM for another two years when I found the opportunity at SUNY New Paltz. I was hired seven years ago in a brand new position as a

Financial Analyst for SUNY. In 2010, my son left for the Navy and I found myself alone. I had lived with my parents up to when my son left for the Navy as I felt it gave him stability and a male role model that he wouldn't have had otherwise. After my son left, I decided to move closer to work (I lived almost 30 miles away from the college). I bought a house in Port Ewen in 2010, my first time living alone in my 46 years. It was both challenging & exciting and very nice to have something to call my own. At the end of 2011, I met Chris; we met through e-harmony. October 2013 was one of the most memorable months of my life, Chris asked me to marry him, my granddaughter was born, and I was promoted to Assistant Vice President of Budget at work. I gradually went from being in an abusive relationship, raising a son alone and having no money to an Assistant Vice President with a good marriage, and a stable life-style. I did the best with whatever I had at the time. I worked hard, stayed focused and made sure I had goals. It took me 25 years to get here, but here I am. I truly believe sharing this helps more people out of the dark and we all need to know we are not alone. Thanks for letting me share.

Sharon - Waterville, WA

I was unable to go to my sailor's graduation for financial reasons and a back injury that makes driving long distances hard. My son knew and understood, but it was still very hard. I stayed home and watched the live feed with tears falling the entire time.. I watched as "Liberty" was called, and all the families rushed to get their hugs. I felt like I was letting my son down. Ironically, just as the live feed shut down, the

FedEx man knocked on our door and delivered his official pictures. This was the only hug I was going to get (hugging his picture). He graduated Oct 11th 2013 and came home for Christmas that year. I stood at the gates and anxiously waited for him to come in the doors! I finally got that long awaited hug!

Kathy - Wichita, KS

Last year, at the age of 48, my husband left me. This day was also the day that I dropped my daughter at the recruiter's office to leave for Boot camp. I have never cried so hard in my life. I knew he had a recent drug problem, but thought we were working through it. I then found out he had cleaned out all my money by stealing my debit cards. I filed for divorce which was final in July 2013. The next six months was a nightmare trying to get my life straightened out. My sailor has since had two accidents in the Navy; one losing part of her thumb which was traumatic on both of us. I turned 50 this past July and even through I have issues with Lupus and Diabetes, I am with God's help better then I have been in a very long time.

Diane - New Boston, NH

Donna B. submitted a story about Diane who has climbed all of New England's 4,000-foot mountains with her two children. Her daughter was the youngest member of the 4,000 Footers Club at one point. Diane now is climbing them again at the age of 44. Adam is ten and well on his way. Diane hiked these mountains with just her kids because her husband worked most weekends, so she had no one else to go with. There were a few overnight hikes where she had to pitch a tent in the woods to sleep. She had some scary nights, wondering when a black bear would perhaps wander over to their tent.

Lori – Lansing, MI

I am Lori. When I was 38, I had been a stay-at-home mom for ten years. Suddenly, a horrible incident happened in my home that prompted me to leave my home and my husband. With my four kids, the clothes on our backs, and my car, we left... My kids at the time were 17, 16, 11, and 10. Because I had a great support system of family and friends, I was able to find a part-time job and a place to stay for the kids and me. After struggling to keep it all together for two years and my oldest two kids moving out, I decided to go to law school! I graduated in 2012, got the perfect job with a state agency, and passed the Bar in 2013. I am attorney with that agency and I am loving life and my job! My youngest child is now a United States sailor and I am one proud momma! This is not where I imagined I would be at 46, but things sure have turned out better than I could have imagined.

Sandy - Sacramento, CA

I don't know how to start, so I will start from my beginning.

I was born to a young 15-year-old mother who married a 20-year-old Airman. Three days after I was born, my father was sent to Vietnam. When he returned my mother had moved on and she was pregnant by another man. My father returned to his hometown in Dayton, Ohio. I did not see my father again until I was 18. My mother went on to drift from one relationship to another. She ended up having five daughters from five different men. Her daughters never lived together because they were all shipped off to live with other relatives. I lived with mother until I was five. From then on, I lived with my grandparents. My mother would take me back from my grandparents, but then when it became too much for her, I was shipped back.

When I was in sixth grade, she "married" the man who became my worst nightmare. He was physically, mentally and sexually abusive to my two sisters and me. At the age of 16, I had had enough and told my entire story to my high school counselor. I went on to live in a foster home with a 63-year-old woman who had six foster teenagers. She is whom I credit the transformation that makes me the person I am today. My mother and I resolved our many differences. I had to accept she would and could never be the mother I wanted, or needed. We became friends. That's all I could get from her.

I went on to marry my high school sweetheart. We had two children and my life seemed set. My husband whom I adored and worshipped was an alcoholic. His alcoholism destroyed our marriage and our family. He thought that because he had the money I would and could never leave. I did. I slept on the floor of my best friend's duplex as I tried to put my life back together. I had done this many times throughout my life.

I met my husband in 1999. He was a single father raising his son. We both worked for the same company in different departments. We had some dear friends who really thought we should meet. After a couple of failed attempts, we finally found a common cause, our children. Our dates were dates as a family. Our two sons became best of friends immediately. My daughter was the third wheel at times but being as she is the same age as my stepson, they had plenty in common. Our three children bonded and still share a very strong bond. My younger son talked his older brother into joining the Navy. They both are Nukes. They went through basic and nuke school together. My daughter just graduated with her BA. My husband and I bask in the successes of our children. We are madly in love with one another. He is my family. With my husband and his son, I've "righted" all the wrongs in my life. I have made a home for all of us. I never sold my children out, and everything we did was for their benefit.

Melissa - Coventry, RI

Here is my story...I was adopted at 13 months old. When I turned about 13 things changed. It was as if my parents didn't know what to do with me once I had a voice. My adopted older brother and sister had been turned over to the state. My dad dropped me off at group home, even though they did not have room for me. I was very innocent and grew up very quickly! I cannot give more information than that, and at 48 - I am still not ready. Many years later, and a trying road, I didn't trust anyone. Some people I trusted, but should not have. The miracle was the day that I gave birth to a beautiful baby girl!! I got married a year later, and yes, another beautiful baby girl was born. My girls changed me and gave me purpose. They made me feel what I should have felt many years ago! So you see I'm not sure if I'm amazing, or it's my girls who made me realize that love is possible, and it's the most amazing feeling you can ever feel. Through all the years of struggles and bad memories, they make it all worth it!

Melanie - Oxford, FL

I have been married twice and divorced twice. I have two children from the first marriage and one from the second. My two older daughters didn't have much of a relationship with their biological father, or their now ex stepfather. When I could not stay in the relationship with their now ex-stepfather, they completely understood and were thankful. We moved out and moved from place to place with me working two and sometimes three jobs. I needed to secure a permanent living place as well as provide them with all they needed for school as well as college savings. When my oldest daughter told me she wanted to join the Navy, I was shocked and scared, but so very proud! She is now a Sailor! My next daughter also decided to join the Navy. When I asked her why, she said, "Because I don't want you killing yourself to put me through college, and my sister deserves to have you around for her as you were for us"! Both of my Sailors have set up a college fund for their youngest sister, to which I also put money in. I think I have raised two wonderful young women. They saw all that I dealt with, and know I would do anything for them, so now they are willing to help their little sister and me.

Sharon – Independence, MO

My parents took us on an incredible journey through life and death. I learned a lot about myself and the importance of having a positive outlook on life. Both of my parents were faced with their own mortality at too young of an age. My siblings and I journeyed with mom through her battle with breast cancer. We were with her when she first started chemo. I will never forget the day she called asking if I would come shave her head. Her hair was falling out and it was driving her nuts. Daddy couldn't do it. It was too much for him to endure. So, I cut her hair. I'll never forget the sound of the first snip I made and the tears dropping from both of our faces. She fought and persevered through her entire war. She held on a lot longer than she probably should have, she was a fighter.

Daddy had Alzheimer's Disease. It slowly and silently robbed him of his entire life's memories, but it NEVER took his soul! As his disease progressed, my sister, Elaine, kept telling me we were going to write a book together about this journey. We never did, but we constantly share and reminisce of his final days. One such story of his last days with us involves a butterfly. Maybe now is a time to share it with the world...

Every Day, Ordinary Miracles...February 2, 2013

What is a miracle? According to Merriam-Webster, a miracle is "an extraordinary event manifesting divine intervention in human affairs". We look for miracles, we long for miracles, and we want to experience the larger-than-life miracles...the changing-water-into-wine miracles. I believe those do exist and I believe people have experienced those. However, I also believe miracles happen every day and often go unseen. I think God touches everyone multiple times during a 24-hour span with a miracle, but we are often unaware, or even so closed-minded to recognize those little whispers. We may chalk them up to coincidences or perhaps fail to completely recognize them altogether.

I have faith that God is with me each day. Some days, that faith is hard to come by and I have to dig down deep to find it. There are many days I wake up and don't even acknowledge the fact that God blessed me with another one on this Earth. I grumble about the weather, the mountain of stuff I have to do, how ungrateful my family is, where am I going to find the money to pay this and that...the laundry list continues. Any of this sound familiar?? I pray for miracles, answers, and the direction I should take. I don't always get the answer I want, or I don't "hear" the miracle. Until one morning, I remembered a little God whisper from a few years back. Allow me to indulge awhile and explain the "whisper miracle" my family experienced.

During the summer of 2010, my siblings and I embarked on quite a journey. It was a journey of joy, a journey of remembrance, and a journey of learning how to say goodbye.

Our father's long battle with Alzheimer's was finally

ending. He was dying. It was time to say goodbye again to one of the greatest men who ever lived. You see, we had already said goodbye years ago to the man who raised us; and we learned to love and appreciate the new man who inhabited his body. His mind was slipping daily; he could not dress himself, feed himself or perform the basic daily duties of life. That summer was the culmination of a marriage that spanned 56 years, 5 children, 13 grandchildren and 2 great-grandchildren. It was the end of an era. Our parents had quite the love affair! Was it perfect? No. Did they have struggles in their marriage? Absolutely! They buried a child. They experienced that horrific event that every parent prays will never happen to them. Somehow, through it all, they came out of that dark time together and intact. They loved each other; there was no doubt. When our mom passed away in 2007, Daddy was devastated. From the moment we laid her to rest, Daddy was ready to join her. He longed for the day when they would be together again. She was his right-hand, his soul mate, but it was not time for him to leave us yet. That summer of 2010 was his last and it was during that summer that we experienced that "whisper" from God. It is a small moment and could have easily been overlooked by us, but thankfully, it was not.

The final week of his life, my sisters, my family and I took vigil at his bedside. Both of my sisters had pretty much moved in with me and we all shared in the joy (and frustrations) of caring for Daddy in his final days. Sometimes it was joyous, but often times it was tedious, frustrating, tiring and heartbreaking. On Wednesday, August 11, 2010, we had taken a break and were sitting outside on the back patio. We were talking, reminiscing and laughing when we noticed a butterfly in the yard. We did not give it a second thought until it fluttered up underneath the patio overhang. The butterfly (a common Monarch butterfly, nothing fancy) danced and flitted, and then it briefly flew over each of our heads. We sat there mesmerized and joking and waving "Hi" to the butterfly, like three little giddy schoolchildren. This only lasted for a few moments, and then the butterfly flew away. We looked at each other and immediately ran inside the house...we thought maybe Daddy had passed and the butterfly was his way of saying goodbye. We realized Daddy was still alive and just chalked up the incident as something funny...we were so very, very wrong!

Over the course of the next few days, a butterfly visited each one of us frequently. Once, during one of its visits to me, the butterfly even buzzed over my parent's dog, almost as if saying "Hi". Another time a butterfly visited me on the back porch, flew over to the back door, and hovered for a while. It almost seemed that the butterfly wanted in the house. These visits began to bring us a sense of peace. We began to talk about these visits and started to wonder if God was trying to say something to us.

On August 15th, Daddy's final day with us, one of my sisters was sitting at his bedside. She looked out of his window and there was a butterfly resting on the bush that sat underneath. It was as if it was beckoning Daddy to join it. My sister left his bedside and within a half-hour, he took his final breath. We were filled with a mixture of emotions...relief, joy and sadness. Our parents were gone and we were now the older (and wiser) generation. What an overwhelming thought!

As I went outside to take in the events, I looked across the street. I saw the most amazing sight…TWO butterflies were flying away together. They were circling each other in a dance of joy, as if they were long lost friends. I stood there transfixed for what seemed like hours, but I am sure it was only a few moments.

Those butterflies and visits meant something-but what? Was it mom visiting us? Were the two butterflies dancing away together reuniting Momma and Daddy? I doubt it. Over the years, I have thought back to those precious moments and asked those same questions.

On my drive in to work recently, I had an epiphany. We experienced a miracle! Not an "in-your-face" miracle but rather one that gently whispered in our ears "I am with you, you are not alone." I believe that God used those butterflies to show us that there is life after death AND there is hope, even in the bleakest of times. What better creature to use than the butterfly? I know that God used those butterflies to bring us comfort, but also to assure us that He has welcomed Momma and Daddy into his Kingdom for eternity. I am so grateful we had an open-mind and were able to see and experience the miracle. How many other miracles have I overlooked? I can assure you, there have been many miracles I have not recognized. I plan to keep my mind; heart and soul open to those regular, everyday occurrences and listen for those God Whispers!

Linda - Sacramento, CA

I started my first day of college in August 1991 at the age

of 40. This was after hearing I was not college material, it was a waste of time and money, and I should just find a job and get married. I was fresh out of a messy divorce that left me scared with the lack of self-worth, confidence, and despair. I had recently lost two jobs due to the lack of computer knowledge. I packed up all my precious stuff and moved 100 miles from familiar territory, to be closer to my children's father, my former husband. I had no idea what college life was going to be, or what living in a new city would bring. All I knew was I did what I was told, believed what I was told, and did not have an opinion that had any value for many, many years. I soon learned I had higher expectations for myself than I realized. When an instructor handed me one of my first graded assignments, I had garnered 24 points out of 25. I knew I had high expectations and I wanted to achieve them.

I started out as a business major in a local junior college. Office work was what I had done in the past and it was all I could do now, so I thought. I overheard two women talking about a class they were enrolled in. It sounded interesting, and I asked what they were studying. The instructor enrolled me and I only learned one thing in the 18 weeks that I sat in that classroom. I learned that people were actually paid to do many of the things that I did as a volunteer; a classroom mom, Girl Scout leader and trainer, baby-sitting co-op coordinator, lunch program director, and religious group leader. I was an organizer, a planner, a skilled coordinator and never knew it! I changed my major to Leisure and Recreation the following semester and was awarded two scholarships along the way. I received my Associates degree in 1993 with a 3.85 GPA. Yeah me!

While in school, I scraped and lived off the interest from the sale of the family home before having most of the proceeds eaten by taxes. I ate Top Ramen 50 different ways and took in a roommate to help me to squeak by. I went without medical insurance, wore thrift store clothes, and took the bus to school to save on gas money. I worked during the summer and Christmas holidays to save up benefits. After the 52-week program ended, I found a 30 hour a week job while still taking 15 to 18 units at college. I also found a mentor, my supervisor, and a woman who traveled the path I was learning to follow. She helped me instill confidence in myself, she helped me build my self-esteem, and most of all she valued my skills and abilities. She forged a great career for her and her two children, and I followed her footsteps. She showed me I had much to offer in a very challenging career and believed in me. I rose up the ladder of the profession, building my own style and presentation. I slowly began to step out of my comfort zone and apply for more responsible and rewarding positions. Along the way, I was able to purchase a small humble home, a "new" used car, and take a real vacation. After being in the health care field for over 20 plus years, I have established a good reputation in the community and have been recruited by local companies to work. I learned:

You cannot always get what you want, but you get what you need.

I can dine with my two most favorite men, Ben & Jerry, and not be yelled at

I can quilt until 1 AM and not criticized

I can set my alarm for 3 AM to see the lunar eclipse

I can go to bed at 8:00 and sleep peacefully

I can spend money and not hear, "you didn't earn it, and you owe me"

I can take a vacation to nowhere with nobody and do nothing without hearing how I waste time and money

I can make mistakes and not be laughed at

I can have success and failures, and not hear you could have done better

I have overcome the "coulda, shoulda, whoulda" disease without medication.

I learned that I have value.

I learned I have friends because of who I am and not because I was somebody's wife.

I learned I have a lot to offer and I can choose who gets what.

I learned I can have a good job with a nice salary

I learned that a national known leader would hire me as a consultant for my skills.

I learned to dream even though I was told dreams were stupid.

First in my journey of learned lessons, I learned to trust. Trust myself, trust others, and choose whom I can trust. After being betrayed by a best friend and confidant who took me under her wing when I left my husband, I learned not everyone is worthy of my trust. After learning, she and he were having a yearlong affair; it hurt to see through their front window, a "family" having fun. I learned no matter what I did or said; my life was changing before my very eyes. I was to travel this journey by myself. I learned that even though they married, she could never be their mother. I am valued and loved by my children. I learned to trust my gut, make mistakes, to take responsibility, and most of all nurture me. I keep on learning and there is no stopping me!

Kathleen - Branson, MS

I was born in a small fishing town in the North of England to poor working class parents. I put myself through nursing school, which is very difficult to do in England. When I started, I knew I was going to be leaving my home and traveling for a while before I settled down and got married. I completed my nurse training and applied for two jobs, one in South Africa and one in Fort Worth, Texas. I arrived in Texas on July 22nd, a nice hot summer day, when I left the North of England it was 57 degrees. I didn't know what I was getting myself in for. I arrived, had a job and a suitcase full of clothes, nothing else! I had just passed my 23rd birthday three months before.

I worked as an RN on the night shift and enjoyed every second. Little did I know I was about to meet my future husband. I was dating his best friend. He was also to become my very good friend; he would come to me when he had girlfriend problems. I went back to England for a year, my maternal grandmother was ill... I took care of her until she passed away. Not long after I came back to the USA living in Little Rock, Arkansas. All this while my good friend and I kept in touch, when I had surgery he invited me to Colorado where he was in school. Well one thing led to another and we got married in   August. We moved back to Texas to be close to his family.

I continued nursing and he had to drop out of school.

Within 3 years, we got the joyful news our family was going to be growing. A healthy baby boy was born! Then along came six years of pain and tears and had four miscarriages. We were lucky to have one child! I was diagnosed with early menopause and told I wouldn't be able to have any more children. God had a different plan in mind. I was pregnant again and had many misgivings; I did not want the pain of losing yet another baby. Joy of joys, another healthy son was born to us. Three years of happiness and fun as our little family grew up. Then tragedy struck again, my 37-year-old husband was diagnosed with Stage 5 Pancreatic Cancer and was told he had six weeks to live! He told the doctors that he wasn't going to die before he was 38, but they said that would be impossible. His family refused to believe what was happening and wouldn't help me in any fashion.

My family was in England, so there I was with a three year old, a ten year old, a full time job and a dying husband. Thanks to my Church, they had a schedule of families willing to help me with the children when I had to rush to the hospital with my husband. His birthday came and went and he was still with us, sadly, he went into a rapid decline when he reached his birthday. My children had to watch their dad go from 230 lbs. to 99 lbs. in six months. By Thanksgiving, I had to take off work to take care of him, as he couldn't do anything for himself. He finally passed away just about a month after his 38th birthday, on Pearl Harbor day.

I was widowed for five years raising hellions of boys who were angry at the world. My in-laws pretty much accused me of killing their son. They filed a lawsuit to try to get custody of my children even though they had no legal reason. The only thing they had going for them was the "good old boy network" in Fort Worth. They called Child Protective Services three times, for neglect twice and for sexually abusing my youngest every night in bed and saying they had witnesses to prove it. Of course, I was cleared each and every time and filled out the forms to have my name removed from their computer files. They had me followed and tapped my phone. My life was pretty much a living h*ll. I had over $55,000 of debt from medical bills. I raised my boys with the best of my abilities for those five years. I met my new husband and married and we moved two states away from the old in-laws. They were toxic to the children and me. I must have done something right when I was raising my sons. My eldest informed me he was joining the Navy, he was older than the usual so it was a surprise. My youngest son informed me he wanted to become a Marine; he was 17. I told him if he could graduate high school and get at least 15 hours of college with a GPA of 3.5, I would sign the forms. Well I never thought that would happen, but of course he did it. My eldest went to Great Lakes to Boot camp on December 5th and my youngest went to Parris Island to Marine BC on January 12th. Both of my sons in boot camp at the same time, I only thought that was harrowing. My youngest was offered Presidential Guard detail, but he said he became a Marine to be in the Infantry. He was sent to a combat unit and stationed at Kaneohe Bay, in HI. The eldest decided that he was going to try for a sibling co-location request and he went to a Destroyer at Pearl Harbor, HI. Wow, both my kids so far away but that was only the beginning. Within a year, my youngest was off to Afghanistan and spent his 19th birthday there. My eldest son also deployed during that time, somewhere near the China Sea. In a three-year period, I only had both of my children on U.S. soil together for about six months. I always had one or the other or both of them deployed. I aged overnight. I was known by my name at the Post Office because I sent at least two packages every day for months. My youngest came back from Afghanistan for the second time two months before he turned 21. He is now out of the Marines and doing well in the civilian world. My eldest is a Corpsman currently assigned to an aircraft carrier and is actually on the same land mass as I am. He spent two years at the hospital in Rota, Spain as a Navy Corpsman. To say I am proud of my children would be an understatement, but the adversity that they endured during their childhood has made them into wonderful young men, with a very much stronger and wiser mother. I hope this story has helped in understanding how families can cope with their children becoming heroes and defending their country. Thank you for allowing me to tell my tale.

Jessie - Irmo, SC

When my children were little I worked part time. When I divorced, I found myself desperate for a job. I took a very menial, labor-intensive job with a government contractor while finishing my Paralegal degree. A different contractor purchased our contract in 2009. My manager at the time had a friend who was still a manager at Palmetto; I was involved in establishing their program for participating in Administrative Law Judge hearings on Medicare denials. However, when they lost that contract I lost the job.

RIF notices were handed out on June 13 of 2013. My dad was diagnosed with Stage 4 throat cancer that month. The prognosis was decent, he would take a trial drug for six weeks and then have surgery, followed by "a little radiation" if needed. My last day of work was a Friday in September and his surgery was the following Wednesday in Charleston, SC. We live about 90 miles away, in Columbia. So really, the timing was not terrible because my severance package allowed me to be out of work short-term to help with his recover, and keep the bills paid. However, the job market was poor and all of my work experience has been with Medicare appeals, a small niche. I sent out hundreds of resumes with only a handful of responses. It was discouraging to say the least. There has been in a long, drawn out, self-created and somewhat delusional battle with my brother and his ex-wife. He and I stopped speaking years ago when I refused to write an affidavit supporting him as the custodial parent of their son. His rage extends to all women but in particular, his ex-wife, and sometimes me. Other times he loves me, as a brother should. I guess it depends on his meds. He had told our friend that he realized he would never see his son again as they had moved to Boston, MA and he could not afford child support or travel. He had nowhere to go except my dad's couch and "may as well go on a killing spree". He would kill all the women who had wronged him, starting with his ex and coming back for me. Extremely irrational. This was just before my dad's surgery. I went to my dad and expressed to him that I thought we needed to call probate, the court that handles involuntary commitments. My dad told me if I did that, he would never speak to me again. I did it anyway. My brother has never been violent, but if he HAD hurt someone, I could not live with it. The paramedics and police went to pick him up, and he and my dad sat there watching TV just like any father/son would do, and the police had no reason to take him in. He said his words were misunderstood. His words were (so he said) "my ex makes me so mad sometimes I could kill her" but he explained that he would never hurt anyone. It was just a figure of speech. I know that he had an elaborate plan but thank God, he never acted on it. He did become angrier with me than ever. He had to leave my dad's house when my dad was coming out of the hospital because my dad had a trachea and feeding tube and multiple wound sites that needed to be cared for, and he needed around the clock care. My brother was absolutely, mentally, not capable. We told him he had to leave and he went on a binge drunk, then called his psychiatrist where he was placed in a psychiatric unit for a few weeks, ultimately being released to a shelter until he was able to find work and a rental. This was a mess for a man who had at one time been extremely successful in business! Backing up, my dad's surgery the following week was brutal. He went to the premier hospital for head and neck cancer, and they almost killed him multiple times. I spent days and days at the hospital. I missed my younger son's 14th birthday because I couldn't leave my dad. I went days without showers! I was jobless anyway. During that time, the company I had worked at while finishing my degree listed a job that I was now perfectly suited for, because of both the work I had done at Palmetto GBA and my Paralegal degree. I applied and came in for an interview. It was like coming home! The interview was a formality because my manager called me just a few hours later with an offer, which almost doubled the salary I was making before I left. I always tell my kids and I truly believe that if you do WHATEVER it is you have to do, to the very best of your ability, and give more than is asked, it will come back to you. In my case it did. Remember, my old manager recommended me for the job that made me eligible for the job I have now. If you are following this story, you are amazing because reading over it; it is very hard to follow. Have I mentioned how much I love my job? I have the most amazing manager and co-workers, the work is interesting and meaningful and the company truly appreciates all that we do. Karma has been kind to me! I mentioned my depper getting in some trouble...he had a trespassing charge his senior year of high school. He also had very poor grades. He came close to not graduating. When he swore in, he self-admitted to smoking pot in high school. His job will be Boatswain's Mate and he is extremely disappointed and discouraged. He had his heart set on being a Hospital Corpsman, and his ASVAB was 89 which I hear is pretty good, and had he not done the stupid things he did, he could have his pick of jobs, but now he will have to get there the hard way. I have cried for him, but there is a lesson there. I hope he follows my example of hard work and perseverance. I cannot imagine ending up in a better place, professionally. I think if he works hard, he will too. I tell him that the men and women enlisting in those jobs put in their time in high school, while he was playing, and so he has to start at the bottom. He has been a good sport, is working out, working 40 hours a week, helping around the house and generally getting himself prepared. I am proud of how he's handled the disappointment. I had said repeatedly to him…the choices you make today MATTER, but he didn't listen. NOW he hears! To finish the story…my dad turned 82 this August. He amazes me. He has never regained the ability to swallow, but other than that, he just keeps on going. He goes to baseball games, volleyball games, theater, goes out to dinner with friends (of course without eating). I know he won't be here forever but he is making the most of what he has left. My brother is waiting tables somewhere in Georgia. Occasionally he comes to visit my dad, and I make a point to show up too, because it makes dad happy to see us together. We really don't like each other much, but we fake it.

Cindy -
Contributor prefers not to have city or state revealed

I have been with many people as they are close to death. Many nights I would sit beside the bed of a person fixing to take their last breath and it was a pleasure and an honor to be beside each one. One case in particular was a soldier that fought in a war. I got to know this great man very well in the weeks I took care of him. He had dementia and many days would talk about his time during war. Some days he would talk about friends that he made while in the Army. His family told me that he lost quite a few friends during the war and always felt guilty because he did not do more to save them. Why did they die there and he did not? Some days he would get very agitated and I believe he was, in his mind, back trying to save someone.

I can usually tell when the time to die is drawing close,

the soldier was suffering, and we would call the family in to say their goodbyes but the soldier would defy all odds and pull through and continue to suffer. His family kept saying, "Dad it's ok, you can go home now", but the soldier never seemed to "let go". Sometimes people have unfinished business and will hold on for days or even weeks until they make peace with a person or event. I began to feel this was the case with this Soldier. I discussed this with his family and they felt that their dad had never gotten over trying to help his friend during the war. After much discussion, the son decided that his dad needed to have orders from his "Army superiors" and he stood in front of his dad and said, "Good Job Soldier, You have received your orders to go home." Three hours later the Soldier passed in peace.

Deborah - Mocksville, NC

It was in April, 1998 when Mark, my husband of eight years, chose to leave me and our three sons, ages six, four, and nine months for what, I suppose, he considered greener pastures. While I was dealing with the stress and fallout from this, I found a lump in my left breast. I was only 31 years old at the time and there was no family history of breast cancer, so I was not worried a great deal about it. I saw my doctor and she wasn't too concerned about it either, but insisted I see a general surgeon for a biopsy just to be sure. I remember well the giddy, drunken feeling I had coming out of the anesthesia. I remember the crash when I heard the words "Yes, it's cancer". Not only was I looking at a future as a single mom, but now I was faced with disfiguring surgery and chemotherapy while fighting a life threatening disease. I was a total wreck and I felt like God had abandoned me. While all of this was going on, a man that I had known my whole life and a life-long childhood friend of my Dad had also been diagnosed with cancer. His nickname was Bull and his cancer was terminal. It was through Bull, a decade earlier, that I had met Vann, his stepson. I was only 21. We dated for a while and were head over heels about each other at the time, but I was put-off and down right scared that Vann was in the Air Force Special Forces; so I panicked & ended it -not my finest moment. Vann had recently moved back up to NC from Florida to be closer to his mom and Bull. He had left the Air Force and was now an Air Traffic Controller with the FAA. Behind the scenes, Vann, having heard about my health issues, was asking my Dad about me. Apparently he asked my Dad often enough that my Dad finally told him, "If you're so concerned about her, go check on her yourself". It took him a while, but in January 1999, he did. Mark had just picked up the boys for his Wednesday evening visit when someone knocked on the door. I answered, fully expecting to see Mark there having forgotten something, but Vann was standing there instead. He asked me out to dinner - I accepted. It was the first of many dates. Considering our history together, my heart knew quickly that this was serious but I was worried about how my cancer and my kids would affect the relationship. Due to the lingering effects of chemo, I was still bald during the first couple of months that Vann & I were together. The day that I threw caution to the wind and took off my wig in front of him was a big deal for me. I was exposing what I considered a weakness, a major fault to him...and I was terrified. When Vann, without missing a beat, put his arms around me, smiled and said, "My God, I've fallen in love with Curly"; I knew that it was forever. He was with me as I finished my treatments and had my final surgery. I was with him through Bull's final months and death in April 1999. Vann had never married and was a 37 year old bachelor when we wed in October 1999. He immediately became "Poppy" to my three rambunctious boys. However, he truly wanted a child of his own. It became the topic of many discussions we had over the next year. We finally spoke with my doctors about it, knowing that the chances were slim that I would be able to conceive after chemotherapy. The doctors confirmed that while it was not impossible, it was not probable. We were told not to get our hopes up and that even if it did happen, it could take a considerable amount of time. Vann & I decided that we didn't want to jump through hoops and go through multiple medical procedures in order to become pregnant. We gave it to God; if it happened, it would be wonderful. We finally got permission to proceed to start trying in June of 2001. Almost immediately, my husband started a daily running "joke", trying to keep things light....asking me "So, are you pregnant yet?" I always returned his smile with a smile, telling him no and reminding him that it was too soon. When my response changed from the usual "no" to a succinct "yes" only four short weeks later in July, of course he doubted me. He thought I had finally had enough of his joking and was just trying to get him to leave me alone. Then I showed him the positive result of my pregnancy test; he was at a loss for words as was I. After only one month, I was pregnant! In March 2002, we welcomed a beautiful, healthy baby girl to our family. She is our miracle baby and I can't help but believe that she is destined for great things in life. Vann & I are still happily married and we celebrate our 11th anniversary in just a few days. He has retired from the FAA. I haven't had to hold a public job since we were married. Two of our sons are grown & supporting themselves, one of those being my Sailor. Our youngest son is a junior in high school where he is considering military service after graduation. Our daughter is a beautiful 12-year-old young person, Jr. Beta Club inductee, volleyball player, choir member & academically gifted straight "A" 7th grader. She is also considering military service, by way of the Naval Academy. Can you tell I am just a bit proud? Yes, I am one very proud, exceedingly blessed wife, mother & woman. Even through my trials, God is good.

Rebecca - Leander, TX

I grew up in a very strong Christian Southern Baptist home. Mom was secretary at the church and played organ, dad was a Deacon. I feel blessed by my upbringing. I dealt with many learning issues growing up which was later diagnosed when I was in my mid 20's as ADD Hypo (aka day dreamer) I graduated high school and went on to college. While in high school, I had to watch my grandfather whom I was very close to slowly fade away from a stroke and pass away the summer before my senior year in high school. I went on to finish my senior year without my grandfather. I went off to college on a full band scholarship for Tuba! While in college, I met who I then thought was the love of my life and started dating.

Because I did not have the structure growing up, I started failing by mid second semester. I had sunk into my first round of deep depression. I went home to seek help. I continued to date whom we will call Bob (not his real name) and after a year, we got engaged. We found out on our first anniversary we were expecting. We were both excited and scared. Our son came along June of 1997.

Soon after, I slowly started to see a change in Bob. At the time, I didn't know it but what he was doing was verbal abuse. I said I was going to leave and I remember him being on the phone with his dad and walking out to my car and doing something to make it not start I also remember running across the street with the baby while he tried to convince me I was imagining things. Over the next two years I was told if I ever left, he would take the one thing that meant the world to me....my son. Finally, it came down to me not caring if I lived or died. My family and friends thought I had the perfect marriage, if only they could see behind the closed doors of our home they would have understood the pain I was in and the abuse I suffered. No one heard him calling me a "fat cow". No one saw him drag me to the bedroom by my hair to "do as a wife should". No one saw the pillow shoved over my face smothering me; no one saw the knife he raised at me because there was never a mark left. But there was a mark that no one can see that still here 16 years later; the mark of "no one will ever want you", "your ugly", "you're crazy" -that tape recorder has yet to break in my mind. I finally broke down and realized "I NEEDED HELP". I was placed into a mental hospital because I no longer wanted to live. I was hiding in my closet doing self mutilation, taking my rings and scratching my arms, hitting my head as hard as I could on anything and, pulling my hair out. ANYTHING to stop the pain he was causing me. Every time this sweet little boy would come find his mamma and sing, "You are my sunshine". It was at that point I knew I needed to live and fight for him. I remember sitting in my doctors office in the fetal position and Bob, acting like the loving husband and, "oh I care so much -I'll do whatever it takes to make you better" - never once admitting he was the reason I was there! They sent me out of state to a mental hospital so he couldn't find me or have access to me. I went home a month later changed more of the person I used to be - I went home with a plan to attend college. Bob said I was selfish and only thinking of myself. I came home to my beloved dog given away. I came home to my home foreclosed on and Bob taking what he wanted out leaving me to empty the house of the rest of my things. I came home to find all the journals I had written about my memories of my grandfather GONE. My last gift from my grandfather my class ring GONE. I ended up back in the hospital for another mental breakdown. I came back the second time to find he had filed for divorce and custody of our son. After a year-long battle in court, I lost custody and was granted supervised visits- I was mentally unstable. I could not prove abuse, because I had no police reports because there were no marks he was never charged. There are days I wish he had just punched me and given me a black eye or some type of mark because no one see's the scars on the inside of the soul. I have moved on with my life, but I still fight the demons he has caused in my soul. In 2003, I met someone and soon after I got pregnant and he wanted to move back to Texas, so we moved. In 2004, I was blessed with a beautiful little girl, and once again faced mental abuse. He wanted another child and in 2007 and we were blessed with another beautiful little girl. When she was six months old, I found myself a single mom alone with no family or friends. The girl's father was seeing someone else because he wanted a "family". I said I was going to move back to New Mexico and found myself the center of a Child protective service investigation for child neglect. The case was closed shortly because all they saw was a single mom trying her best with two little girls who loved their mom. I had a great job, new car and found myself laid off with money running out. A friend I had met asked me to move in, in 2009, she was also a single mom. Life was looking up FINALLY! Then, one day she decided she didn't want me as a roommate. She made up a story that even my girl's dad told her "no good would come of it." My roommate called CPS on me. I found myself homeless; I had just given her all my cash the day before for rent. I called all my friends and no one could take me in. I remember sitting in the parking lot of Hobby Lobby crying and asking God WHY! I called someone I barely knew that I had met at a bar dancing and he took me in. I remember walking in and falling into his arms feeling broken and deflated, as if someone had just stabbed me in the back. I called my parents to tell them what had happened - I was thrown more bad news. A lifelong family friend I had known my whole life had passed away. That was Sept 17th 2009. I remember standing in front of my only friend in my life and him catching me as I sunk to the ground even more broken. I stayed there and dealt with CPS. I called CPS a few days later advising that I'm not running away -but I JUST NEED TO GO HOME AND FIND MY

STRENGTH! I needed my family and to pull myself together to fight this case because I was looking at possible police charges. I remember getting in my car and driving to Roswell, New Mexico where a friend lived. I fell apart and slept for a long time. I got back on the road to go home to my son and parents. Here I would gain my strength and find the fight I had in me. I ended up staying longer then expected in New Mexico because my grandmother fell and my mother was sick. While there, I got a call about the job interview I had before I had left and had a job waiting for me. I got in my car, contacted a apartment locator, and I found a place to live. However, due to poor credit, I couldn't be helped. I sat there crying in a strangers office with all my possessions in my car. I had no home and no place to go. He gave me a number to another person and said, "Don't give up- call her." I called her and I remember her asking me how much money I had. It wasn't enough. She stood up and gave me a big hug and said, It's going to be ok". This kind woman gave me the difference so I could get a place to live. In December of 2009, I was finally granted unsupervised visits right before Christmas. In 2010, I went on a date that has probably changed my life forever. I used to think the guys in the past were "THE ONE" . Now I think they were building me into the woman I am to day. On March 16, 2010, I went on a date. When he opened the door for me, I just knew I had found my forever man. He puts up with my quirks and is patient with me. I moved in with him in July of 2010. My girls would come over on the weekends. I missed them and wanted them home, I felt guilty some days, but I prayed often that if they were meant to be with me - there would be a way. In August 2010, the girl's dad was in an accident at work and broke his back. In November, 2010, I told my man I wanted my girls home for good. He said, "If that's what you want, that's how it will be." We sat down and talked with girl's dad and stepmom and decided they were thriving and doing well in this environment - so they would stay with me. You might be asking yourself well what about her son....I talked to him daily when he was growing up. I wrote this for Face Book to explain the situation in 2011. Many people ask me why he doesn't live with me because after all I am his mom. To understand we must go back! When his dad and I married, it was perfect! Then slowly the verbal and some physical abuse started. Long story short I could not take it anymore and didn't care if I lived or died. When I reached that point, I knew I needed help, so I sought out help. I ended up seeing a Psychiatrist or psychologist (something psych LOL) they decided the best thing for me was to go into a "MENTAL HOSPITAL"! I found my way out...I spent a month there getting my mind better! I came home to find he had filed for divorce and custody of our three-year-old son. When it was said and done, the man that put me there got put in custody...He used the fact that I was in a "loony bin" against me and said I was an unfit mother. The whole time I kept telling him I was planning on leaving. He would tell me, "If you leave me, I'll take the one thing that means more to you than anything." I stayed - and never left until I hit my breaking point of being in a mental hospital. I never thought for once I would lose...I mean, I am the one that took care of him day in day out night after night for 3 years, it was not his dad but me. So at four years of age my son was forced to go live with his dad. I rarely spoke to his father after that day all communication went through my parents. I saw my son as often as I could. At age five or six, I can remember him coming up to me and saying "Mom I know that it's not that you don't want me, I know it's because of my daddy I can't be with you". SERIOUSLY!! At a young age, he was just too smart! I never once badmouthed his dad, I never told him what truly happened, and he comes to me and says that….I cried! For the longest time until he got into his teens, he would always tell me, "I love you to the moon and back". Oh, he melts my heart when he says that! Guess he is too old for it, but I still tell him. He starts the game of , "I love you to the moon and back and around the whole universe". I can't compete with that….that's a lot of love from a boy who I don't see very often.

Over time, I moved on and his dad moved on. I made a hard choice in moving to Texas and leaving him in New Mexico. I heard people comment, "What kind of mother is she?" I was one that needed out…a fresh start! In addition, deep down I knew he was going to be ok and he is! Slowly over time, my son started spending more and more time with my parents. His dad never had time for him - besides that, he was told to watch his younger brother and sister often.

At age 13, he asked to move in with my mom and dad. So to answer the question; "Why doesn't he live with me since he doesn't want to live with dad - and, why don't I fight for custody?" Because as a mom you sometimes have to do what is right for your child! He is an A/B student. Why would I go in and rip him from where he is to prove I am a good mom by taking him back. To me a good mom knows what is best for their child and scarifies their want and desire. I would give anything (well almost) to have him with me, and to see and talk to him everyday in person, and not by phone, Skype or text...but I know I am doing the right thing by leaving him there. So why don't I move back home?? Well that would mean taking two little girls away from their dad, and leaving where I have finally found peace and happiness! Yes, I get homesick, Yes, I miss my family but I also know I am doing well here. I know I took myself away from my son. Yes, I have regrets about it, but I have talked to my son about it and he understands and doesn't hate me for it! So I live everyday with a piece of me missing...I sacrifice for my sons well-being . That my friends, is what a mom does!!! My son will always be what keeps me going. In a way he is my own hero! If it were not for him, in my darkest days - singing; "You are my sunshine", I probably would not be here.

At times, I do not feel I should carry the title Proud Navy Mom because in reality I did not raise him, I did not help shape him into the young man he has become. I struggle some days with that. It was not my choice or my doing. My son and I are close, we have talked about some of the reasons why, and he understands. When something exciting happens I'm who he calls first not his dad, not his grandparents, me - his mom.

I haven't had an easy life- I've had my ups and my downs, but I'm sitting here writing this in the man's home whom I went on my first date on March 16th 2010, my girls are sleeping in the next room, and my son is celebrating one year in the Navy tomorrow. I may not have a car, or a job, but I have a family that loves me even on my dark days when I feel like running. I have a man who accepts the fact that I am broken on the inside from years of mental abuse. I have faith in God that I will get through anything life throws at me.

Kristi – College Station, TX

When the new recruits first arrive at the Recruit Training Command in Great Lakes, IL they go through sleep deprived processing. The recruits quickly learn not ask questions - or even speak. During this processing, they get the clothes that they need for boot camp. When it came time for my daughter to get her undergarments, she knew what size she needed. She said everything was fuzzy and nothing was labeled clearly. She quickly grabbed the first package that looked relatively close to her size. She grabbed the bag marked "10" and took off down the line. Next, they had to try all the clothing on. There would be no exchanges, but they still had to try everything on. She got down to the undergarments and tried one on. They were excessively big. She looked at the package. The 10 stood for how many were in the package. My daughter, who is a size 6/8, had grabbed a size 14/16 package. No exchanges allowed. She had to wear them all throughout boot camp. The only way she could keep them up was by rolling down the top two to three times. Jumping jacks were nearly impossible!

Sue –
Contributor prefers not to have city or state revealed

Dreams, everyone has dreams! My dream from the time I was nine years old was to work in the medical field. I had been injured and had to go to the emergency room for treatment. It was the way that I was treated when I knew what I wanted to do when I 'grew up.' I was sixteen and dating my boyfriend for over a year, in December of my junior year, I became pregnant and I was due in September. This was the beginning of my senior year of high school. I was stopped in my tracks, as I now had to plan for having a baby. Another dream I had was to graduate high school even if I was going to be a mom. I never entertained quitting school, as I knew that I wanted to work in the medical field, my dream.

My senior year of high school began and I did not attend. I was waiting for the birth of my first child, a son who was born two weeks after school started. I had to figure out how to continue school so that I could graduate. There wasn't an option for me to continue school during the day, as I had no one to watch my son. Living at home with my parents and five siblings, I had the responsibility of caring for my son. I made the choice to continue my education by attending night school to obtain my high school diploma. I began classes in January of the new year, only missing the first semester. There was not one time where it occurred to me to discontinue my education, as I knew I wanted to attend college. I knew where I wanted to go.

My 'boyfriend' and I decided to get married in December, three months after our son was born. I had turned 17 years old in November; he was 18 years old. We had a short service at a local church, though the Pastor had forgotten about it. Could this have been the first omen of something not being right? We broke up for a bit, and then got back together and it was then I got pregnant. Truly, this was not planned so we moved forward with a simple ceremony. Our marriage was not easy; there were many signs that things were not right. Honestly, we were only married for seven months and I knew it was wrong. I stayed because we had our son, now understanding it was for all the wrong reasons.

I earned my diploma, a year later as it took a bit longer with the night school schedule. While going to school, my then husband decided it would be best for him to enlist into the U. S. Army. He went to boot camp and he was stationed in a spot that took us across the country. He had to report the same day as my graduation ceremony therefore I was unable to attend. To this day, have my cap and gown that I never wore.

We were stationed at Fort Ord, California, so far from family in Michigan. The friends I had were going on with their lives and going to college. I was a mom and I was not a part of the circle anymore. This was a tough time for me, but you learn to do what you need to do. I started to work while the husband was in the Army, though certain things started to happen and it was a feeling I had that things were not right and I shouldn't be in this marriage. I stayed because I had my son and I was only 18 years old. We were in California for almost two years before he received orders to go overseas. I decided that I would move back home with my parents and hold down the fort from there. It was a few months later that I decided it was time for me to end the marriage as I knew he would never take me where I wanted to go. Yes, I know it was wrong to write that 'Dear John' letter, but this one was necessary, and it was the right thing to do. The letter was received, the Army sent him home to 'repair' the marriage, but it was over and I have never looked back. I sought out a position in a local hospital and was to be trained as a 'Unit Secretary' that entailed transcribing physician's orders for each patient. I had six weeks of training; I only had one uniform and washed it every day. Moving back to my parent's home and not having a job for about a month, I had to go and apply for welfare. It was a different time in the 70's, nothing like the programs today. I received food stamps once, as I worked I had to send in my pay stubs and only received about a month of financial help.

My parents watched my son on the weekends because I had to work overtime. I lived with a friend, I lived with a cousin then I lived with one of my sisters. I wanted to be on my own, with my son and be able to afford it and not have to move again. After six weeks with my sister, I was able to rent in a Co-Op townhouse community. We had a home of our own and it was a good feeling. I knew I would not need moving boxes again for a while!

Being a single parent, having divorced at 20 years old with a three-year-old son, it was hard to make ends meet. I did not receive child support, though it was court ordered. I learned to depend on no one except myself. Times were not easy, having an ex-husband was not easy, and being alone was not easy. I had dreams; I wanted to go to college. I was now working two jobs because the one at the hospital wasn't enough to pay the bills. I was lucky enough to get a job that was medically related. I took national boards for my job and was now a certified 'Health Unit Clerk Coordinator' (HUCC) and working in the ICU/CCU and learning so much. It was then that I decided I wanted to become a Paramedic. I applied at our local community college for the two-year program. I completed the first year, was two weeks of taking my state boards to be licensed as an Emergency Medical Technician (EMT) and then I was involved in a car accident. I was rear ended by a young inexperienced driver. I do not remember the accident happening, though I can still hear the noise. My car was no longer operable, which caused many problems. I was already working two jobs, working on my clinical hours at the hospital and on an ambulance. I needed a car, so I had to get yet another job (host in a new restaurant opening soon) to earn more money to buy a new one! Yes, now I had three jobs, was attending college and doing my clinical hours. I am not sure how I did all this and care for my son.

Doing some research for a program that would keep me within the medical field that didn't require lifting, I found a private school and applied to a program that would allow me to become a 'Certified Electrocardiogram Technician' (CET). It was not exactly what I had planned nor had a dream to do, but still I would be working in the medical field. I did the program and graduated with honors!

I met a person who was six years younger than I was! What? How could I have a relationship with anyone who was only 11 years older than my son was? God had a plan, it is funny how He presents it to you. Having been single for over eight years, working multiple jobs and going to college, was there even time to start a relationship? I was not sure, but I knew in a short six weeks, that this 'guy' was the right person for me; the one I would love to spend the rest of my life with. I had never felt the way that I was now feeling. Both of us felt it and we got to know each other better. I was a single mother who worked hard and long hours to care for my son. About a year and a half into our relationship 'my guy' proposed, and we were married six months later. We wanted to add to our family, though that did not work out as planned. We had a three and a half year relationship with a fertility specialist, ending it as we concluded that it might be just the three of us after all. I accepted a new position in a hospital not far from our first home we purchased. Three months working at the hospital, it was on Thanksgiving day that we found out that we were pregnant! We were stunned, surprised, excited as well as being scared. We were amazed to see the double line, after all we had gone through we were now expecting a baby! 'My guy' and I went on to have another son. We didn't have as many complications with him as our other son. We were surprised to learn we were pregnant yet again – this time with a daughter. We really had to laugh. My oldest son was married at our home when our daughter was thirteen months old. He and his wife welcomed two daughters in the next three years... Our family had grown. There were 18, 20, 22 years between my oldest son and my younger children. I had a dream long ago of working in the medical field. I got the best job in the world, being mom to three additional children and allowed to stay home for the past 18 years to raise them.

Where are the three younger children? We are now the proud parents of a U. S. Navy son, a U. S. Marine Corps son, and a U. S. Navy daughter. God had a plan, you have to realize that everything is in His hands, in His timing, He shows you the way. We have been very blessed; I have been as blessed as I walked a path that has been quite a journey. It all started with having a dream at nine years old. What is yours? Are you living your dreams, have you overcome obstacles to make your dreams come true. Have you listened to God whisper in your ear of where He wants you to go, to walk, to accomplish. Never stop taking steps to where you need to be, doing what you need to do, to persevere to make your dreams come true. In the end, they may be just the dreams God had planned for you all along. With God's plan, I learned that I did 'amount' to something, someone great! I am worthy, I gave it my all, I succeeded, and in the end, I give all glory to my Lord and Savior.

We all have a story, what's yours?

References

Henderson, E. (2009). *A short history of the honeybee.*
Timber Press: Portland, Oregon.

Interviews and stories from 50 women within the U.S.
(Personal Communication, 2014).

Washington, D. (2006). *A hand to guide me.* Meredith
Books: Desmoines, Iowa.

Wilson, B., (2004). *The hive.* St. Martin's Press: New
York, New York.

Woodbridge, NJ Patch. (2014). Retrieved from:
http://patch.com/new-jersey/woodbridge/
rest-michael-my-son_f64a3166-woodbridges.

Bio

Laura Henderson is a wife, mom, student and working professional. She went back to school later in life and earned her B.S. in Management Studies from Cambridge College. Laura was inducted into the prestigious Sigma, Beta, Delta International Honor Society at the age of 50 – the highest recognition awarded to a business student. Laura is passionate about education and is currently enrolled in the Graduate program at Cambridge College pursuing an MBA where she has based this book as the final thesis project for her degree completion.

Laura and her husband reside in Newburyport, MA.

CPSIA information can be obtained
at www.ICGtesting.com
Printed in the USA
FSOW02n0942081016
25902FS